George Bush

M000020733

Out of Office
COUNTDOWN
HANDBOOK

Hang in there! It's almost over!

SOURCEBOOKS HYSTERIA™
AN IMPRINT OF SOURCEBOOKS, INC.®
NAPERVILLE, ILLINOIS

Published by Sourcebooks, Inc.

P.O. Box 4410, Naperville, Illinois 60567-4410

(630) 961-3900

Fax: (630) 961-2168

www.sourcebooks.com

ISBN-13: 978-1-4022-0904-8

ISBN-10: 1-4022-0904-5

Printed and bound in U.S.

LB 10 9 8 7 6 5 4 3 2

"My pro-life position is I believe there's life. It's not necessarily based in religion. I think there's a life there, therefore the notion of life, liberty, and the pursuit of happiness."

San Francisco Chronicle

2,922 days left

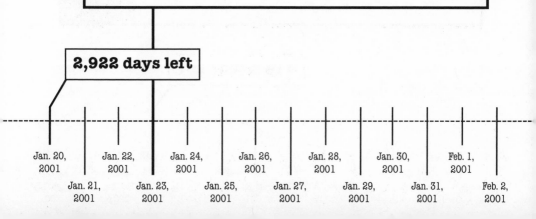

Jan. 20, 2001

Jan. 21, 2001

Jan. 22, 2001

Jan. 23, 2001

Jan. 24, 2001

Jan. 25, 2001

Jan. 26, 2001

Jan. 27, 2001

Jan. 28, 2001

Jan. 29, 2001

Jan. 30, 2001

Jan. 31, 2001

Feb. 1, 2001

Feb. 2, 2001

"I think there is some methodology in my travels."

—*March 5, 2001, Washington, D.C.*

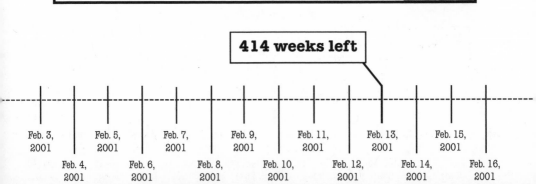

414 weeks left

Feb. 3, 2001	Feb. 5, 2001	Feb. 7, 2001	Feb. 9, 2001	Feb. 11, 2001	Feb. 13, 2001	Feb. 15, 2001	
Feb. 4, 2001	Feb. 6, 2001	Feb. 8, 2001	Feb. 10, 2001	Feb. 12, 2001	Feb. 14, 2001	Feb. 16, 2001	

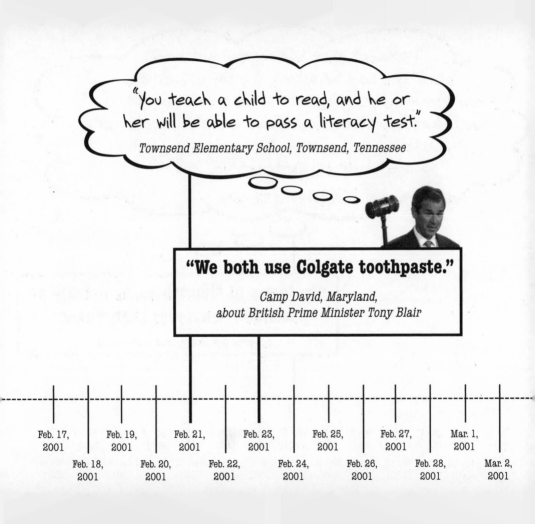

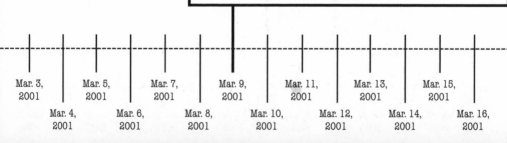

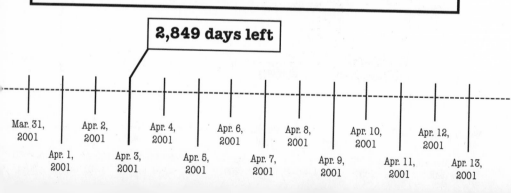

> "And so, in my State of the—my State of the Union—or state—my speech to the nation, whatever you want to call it, speech to the nation—I asked Americans to give 4,000 years—4,000 hours over the next—the rest of your life—of service to America. That's what I asked—4,000 hours."
>
> *April 9, 2002, Bridgeport, CT*

2,849 days left

Mar. 31, 2001 | Apr. 1, 2001 | Apr. 2, 2001 | Apr. 3, 2001 | Apr. 4, 2001 | Apr. 5, 2001 | Apr. 6, 2001 | Apr. 7, 2001 | Apr. 8, 2001 | Apr. 9, 2001 | Apr. 10, 2001 | Apr. 11, 2001 | Apr. 12, 2001 | Apr. 13, 2001

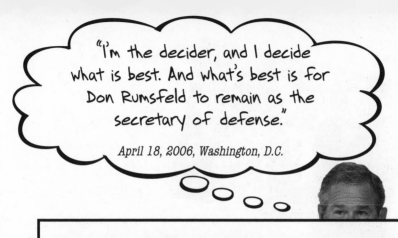

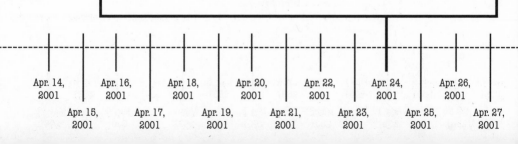

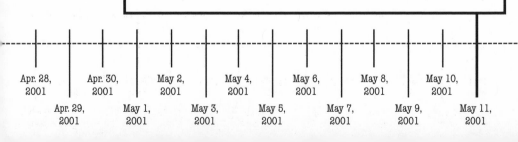

"There's no question that the minute
I got elected, the storm clouds on the horizon
were getting nearly directly overhead."

Washington, D.C.

Apr. 28,
2001

Apr. 29,
2001

Apr. 30,
2001

May 1,
2001

May 2,
2001

May 3,
2001

May 4,
2001

May 5,
2001

May 6,
2001

May 7,
2001

May 8,
2001

May 9,
2001

May 10,
2001

May 11,
2001

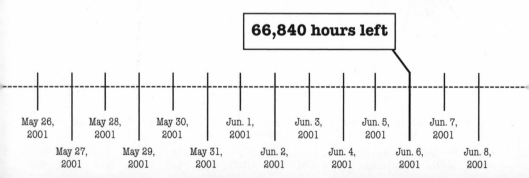

"I'm gonna talk about the ideal world, Chris. I've read—I understand reality. If you're asking me as the president, would I understand reality, I do."

May 31, 2000, on Hardball

66,840 hours left

May 26, 2001
May 27, 2001
May 28, 2001
May 29, 2001
May 30, 2001
May 31, 2001
Jun. 1, 2001
Jun. 2, 2001
Jun. 3, 2001
Jun. 4, 2001
Jun. 5, 2001
Jun. 6, 2001
Jun. 7, 2001
Jun. 8, 2001

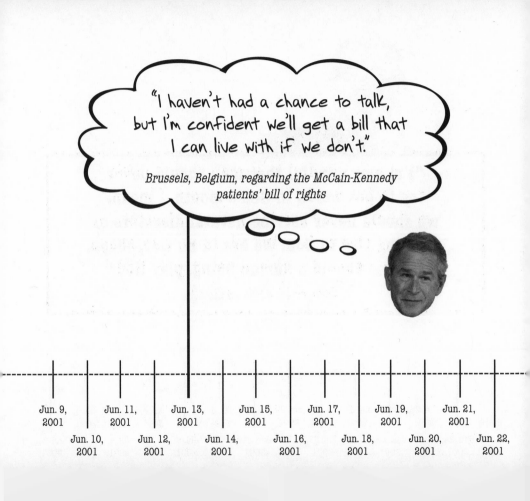

"I'm also mindful that man should never
try to put words in God's mouth. I mean,
we should never ascribe natural disasters or
anything else to God. We are in no way, shape,
or form should a human being, play God."

January 14, 2005, on 20/20

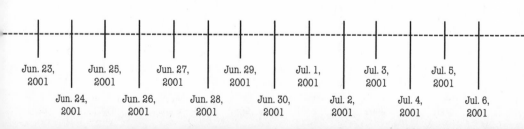

Jun. 23, 2001	Jun. 25, 2001	Jun. 27, 2001	Jun. 29, 2001	Jul. 1, 2001	Jul. 3, 2001	Jul. 5, 2001	
	Jun. 24, 2001	Jun. 26, 2001	Jun. 28, 2001	Jun. 30, 2001	Jul. 2, 2001	Jul. 4, 2001	Jul. 6, 2001

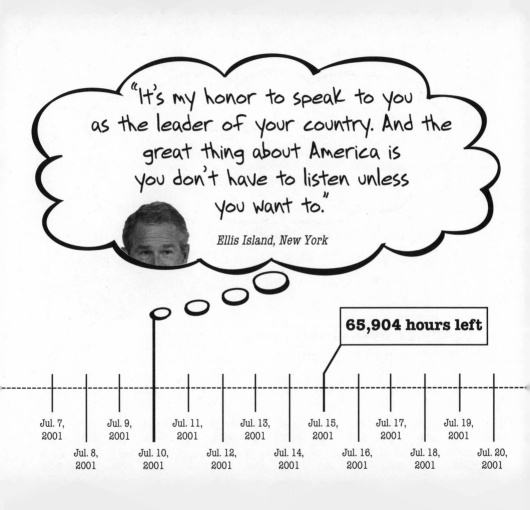

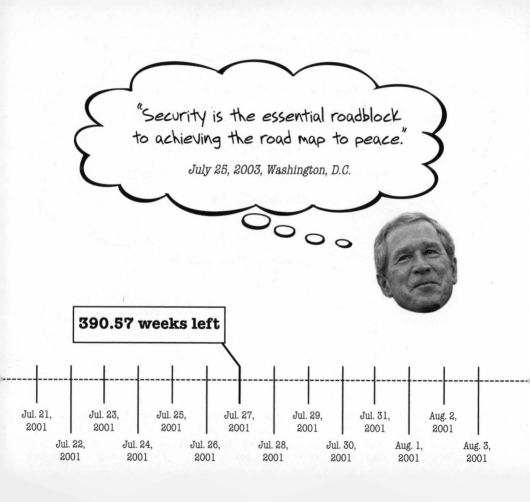

> **"As you know, we don't have relationships with Iran. I mean, that's—ever since the late '70s, we have no contacts with them, and we've totally sanctioned them. In other words, there's no sanctions—you can't—we're out of sanctions."**
>
> *August 9, 2004, Annandale, Virginia*

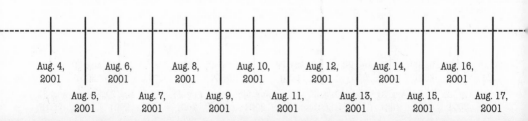

Aug. 4, 2001
Aug. 5, 2001
Aug. 6, 2001
Aug. 7, 2001
Aug. 8, 2001
Aug. 9, 2001
Aug. 10, 2001
Aug. 11, 2001
Aug. 12, 2001
Aug. 13, 2001
Aug. 14, 2001
Aug. 15, 2001
Aug. 16, 2001
Aug. 17, 2001

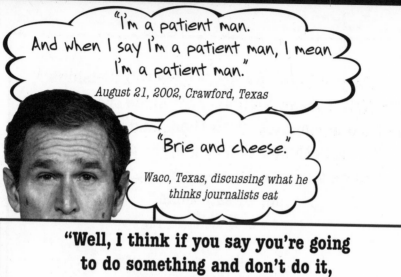

"I'm a patient man. And when I say I'm a patient man, I mean I'm a patient man."

August 21, 2002, Crawford, Texas

"Brie and cheese."

Waco, Texas, discussing what he thinks journalists eat

"Well, I think if you say you're going to do something and don't do it, that's trustworthiness."

August 30, 2000, CNN online chat

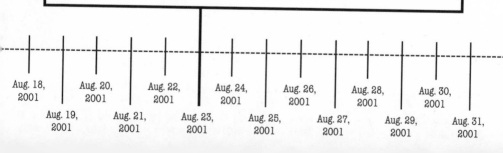

Aug. 18, 2001
Aug. 19, 2001
Aug. 20, 2001
Aug. 21, 2001
Aug. 22, 2001
Aug. 23, 2001
Aug. 24, 2001
Aug. 25, 2001
Aug. 26, 2001
Aug. 27, 2001
Aug. 28, 2001
Aug. 29, 2001
Aug. 30, 2001
Aug. 31, 2001

> **"There's no doubt in my mind that we should allow the world's worst leaders to hold America hostage, to threaten our peace, to threaten our friends and allies with the world's worst weapons."**
>
> *September 5, 2002, South Bend, Indiana*

Sep. 1,
2001

Sep. 2,
2001

Sep. 3,
2001

Sep. 4,
2001

Sep. 5,
2001

Sep. 6,
2001

Sep. 7,
2001

Sep. 8,
2001

Sep. 9,
2001

Sep. 10,
2001

Sep. 11,
2001

Sep. 12,
2001

Sep. 13,
2001

Sep. 14,
2001

"Border relations between Canada and Mexico have never been better."

Press conference with the Prime Minister of Canada

"I'm confident we can work with Congress to come up with an economic stimulus package that will send a clear signal to the risk takers and capital formators of our country."

Washington, D.C.

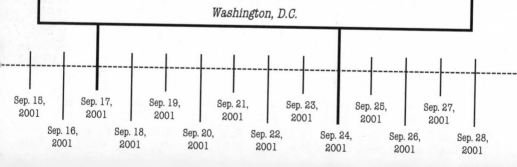

Sep. 15, 2001

Sep. 16, 2001

Sep. 17, 2001

Sep. 18, 2001

Sep. 19, 2001

Sep. 20, 2001

Sep. 21, 2001

Sep. 22, 2001

Sep. 23, 2001

Sep. 24, 2001

Sep. 25, 2001

Sep. 26, 2001

Sep. 27, 2001

Sep. 28, 2001

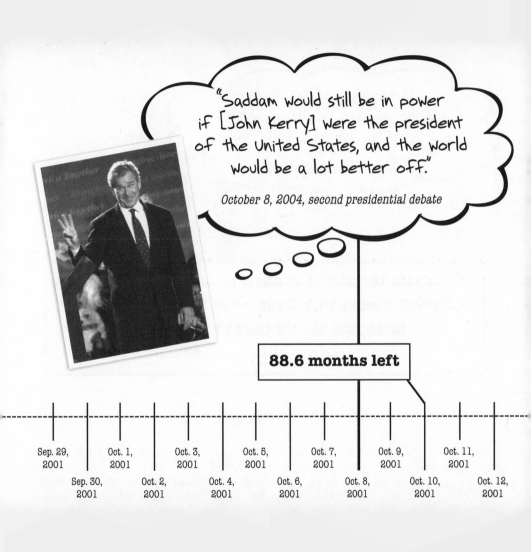

"It's about past seven in the evening here so we're actually in different time lines."

January 2001, Washington, D.C.

"We expect the states to show us whether or not we're achieving simple objectives—like literacy, literacy in math, the ability to read and write."

April 28, 2005, Washington, D.C.

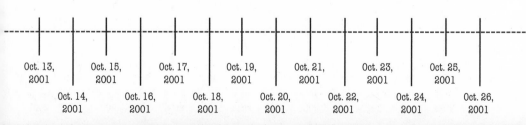

Oct. 13, 2001

Oct. 14, 2001

Oct. 15, 2001

Oct. 16, 2001

Oct. 17, 2001

Oct. 18, 2001

Oct. 19, 2001

Oct. 20, 2001

Oct. 21, 2001

Oct. 22, 2001

Oct. 23, 2001

Oct. 24, 2001

Oct. 25, 2001

Oct. 26, 2001

> **"I need to be able to move the right people to the right place at the right time to protect you, and I'm not going to accept a lousy bill out of the United Nations Senate."**
>
> *October 31, 2002, South Bend, Indiana*

63,264 hours left

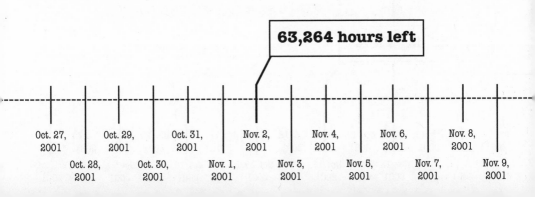

| Oct. 27, 2001 | Oct. 28, 2001 | Oct. 29, 2001 | Oct. 30, 2001 | Oct. 31, 2001 | Nov. 1, 2001 | Nov. 2, 2001 | Nov. 3, 2001 | Nov. 4, 2001 | Nov. 5, 2001 | Nov. 6, 2001 | Nov. 7, 2001 | Nov. 8, 2001 | Nov. 9, 2001 |

> **"The United States and Russia are in the midst of transformationed relationship that will yield peace and progress."**
>
> *Washington, D.C.*

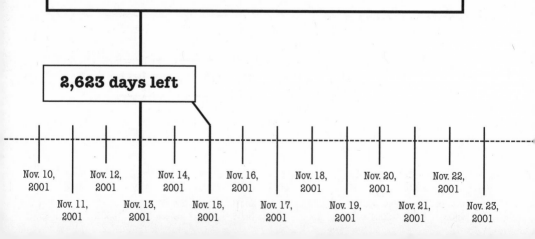

2,623 days left

| Nov. 10, 2001 | Nov. 12, 2001 | Nov. 14, 2001 | Nov. 16, 2001 | Nov. 18, 2001 | Nov. 20, 2001 | Nov. 22, 2001 |

| Nov. 11, 2001 | Nov. 13, 2001 | Nov. 15, 2001 | Nov. 17, 2001 | Nov. 19, 2001 | Nov. 21, 2001 | Nov. 23, 2001 |

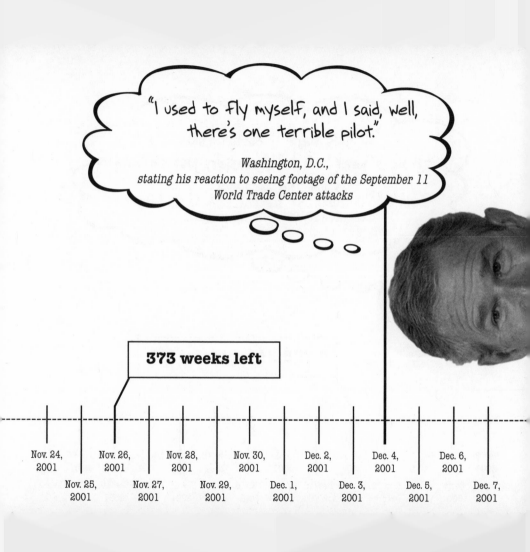

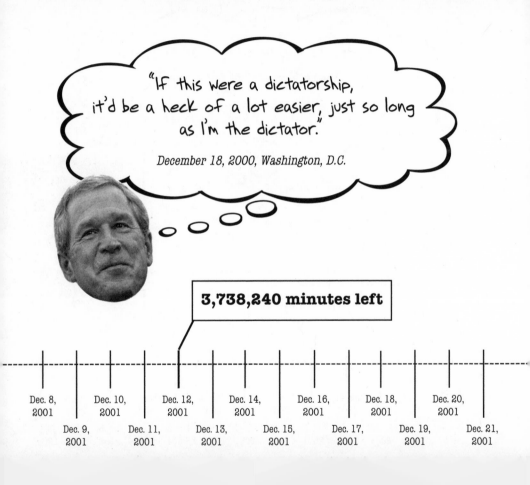

"If this were a dictatorship, it'd be a heck of a lot easier, just so long as I'm the dictator."

December 18, 2000, Washington, D.C.

3,738,240 minutes left

Dec. 8,
2001

Dec. 9,
2001

Dec. 10,
2001

Dec. 11,
2001

Dec. 12,
2001

Dec. 13,
2001

Dec. 14,
2001

Dec. 15,
2001

Dec. 16,
2001

Dec. 17,
2001

Dec. 18,
2001

Dec. 19,
2001

Dec. 20,
2001

Dec. 21,
2001

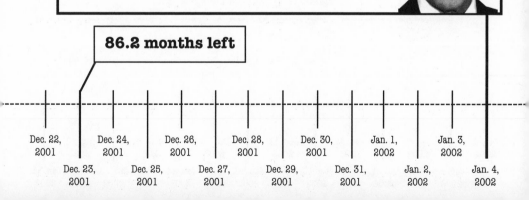

> **"I want to thank you for taking time out of your day to come and witness my hanging."**
>
> *at the dedication of his gubernatorial portrait in Austin, Texas*

86.2 months left

Dec. 22, 2001   Dec. 24, 2001   Dec. 26, 2001   Dec. 28, 2001   Dec. 30, 2001   Jan. 1, 2002   Jan. 3, 2002

Dec. 23, 2001   Dec. 25, 2001   Dec. 27, 2001   Dec. 29, 2001   Dec. 31, 2001   Jan. 2, 2002   Jan. 4, 2002

> ## "You took an oath to defend our flag and our freedom, and you kept that oath underseas and under fire."

January 10, 2006, Washington, D.C.

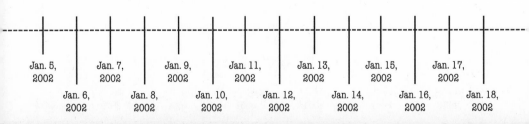

Jan. 5,
2002

Jan. 6,
2002

Jan. 7,
2002

Jan. 8,
2002

Jan. 9,
2002

Jan. 10,
2002

Jan. 11,
2002

Jan. 12,
2002

Jan. 13,
2002

Jan. 14,
2002

Jan. 15,
2002

Jan. 16,
2002

Jan. 17,
2002

Jan. 18,
2002

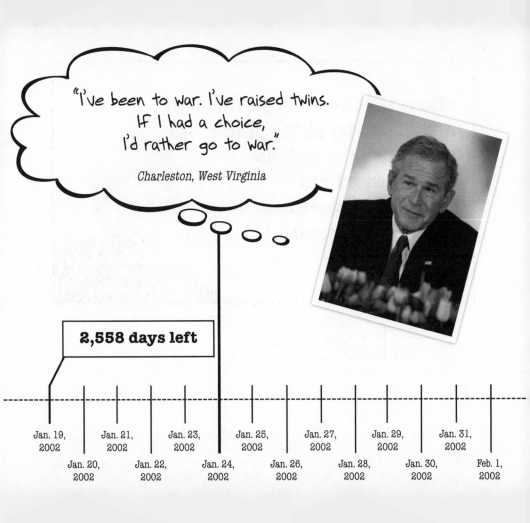

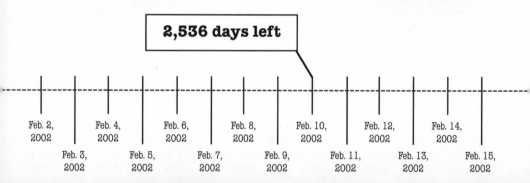

> **"There is no such thing necessarily in a dictatorial regime of iron-clad absolutely solid evidence. The evidence I had was the best possible evidence that he had a weapon."**
>
> *February 8, 2004, on Meet the Press*

2,536 days left

Feb. 2, 2002

Feb. 3, 2002

Feb. 4, 2002

Feb. 5, 2002

Feb. 6, 2002

Feb. 7, 2002

Feb. 8, 2002

Feb. 9, 2002

Feb. 10, 2002

Feb. 11, 2002

Feb. 12, 2002

Feb. 13, 2002

Feb. 14, 2002

Feb. 15, 2002

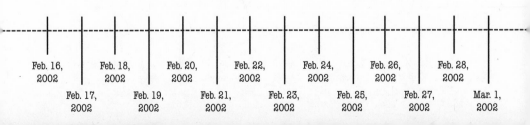

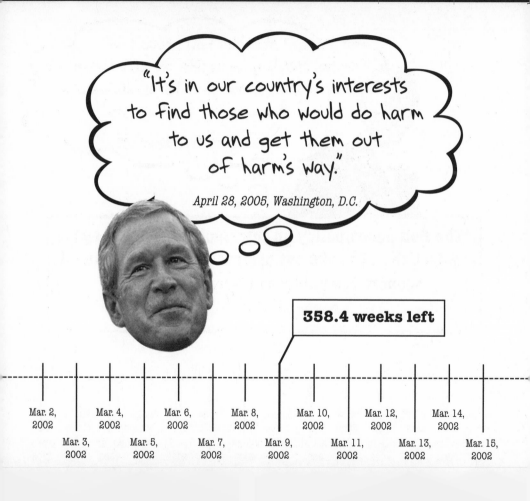

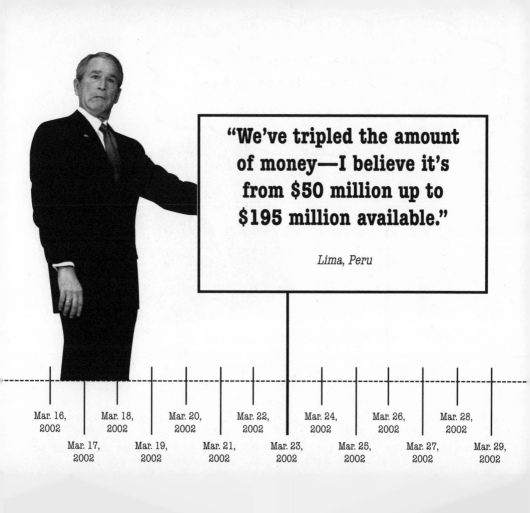

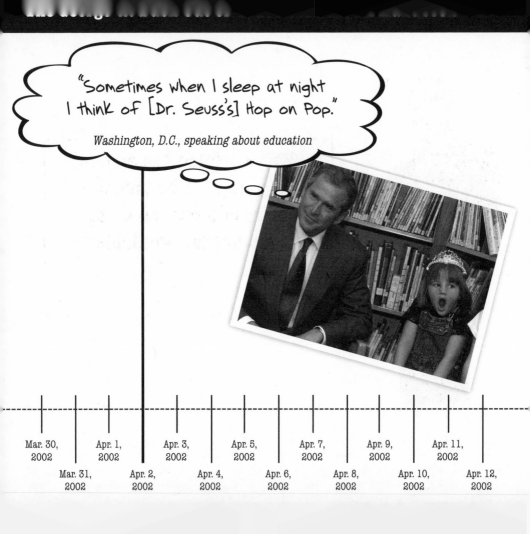

The *San Francisco Chronicle* reports that the White House is removing Bush's mistakes and bloopers from official transcripts of speeches, interviews, and public appearances.

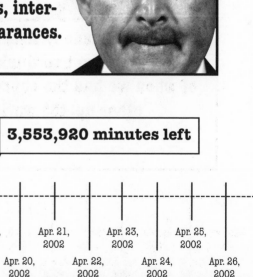

3,553,920 minutes left

Apr. 13, 2002

Apr. 14, 2002

Apr. 15, 2002

Apr. 16, 2002

Apr. 17, 2002

Apr. 18, 2002

Apr. 19, 2002

Apr. 20, 2002

Apr. 21, 2002

Apr. 22, 2002

Apr. 23, 2002

Apr. 24, 2002

Apr. 25, 2002

Apr. 26, 2002

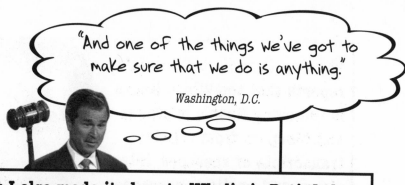

"And one of the things we've got to make sure that we do is anything."

Washington, D.C.

"But I also made it clear to [Vladimir Putin] that it's important to think beyond the old days of when we had the concept that if we blew each other up, the world would be safe."

May 1, 2001, speech in the Rose Garden

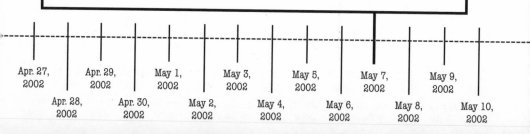

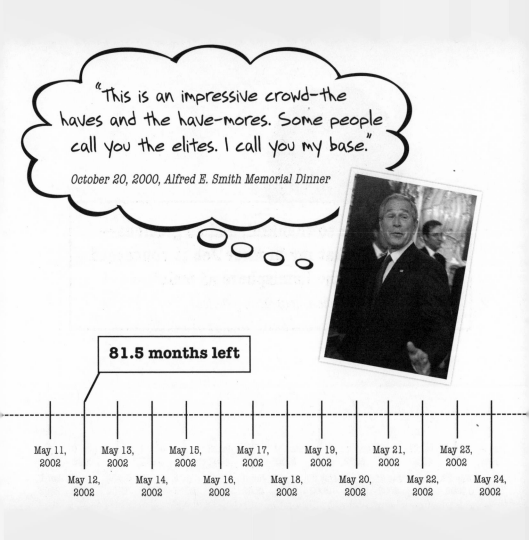

**"Anyway, I'm so thankful, and so gracious—
I'm gracious that my brother Jeb is concerned
about the hemisphere as well."**

June 4, 2001, Miami, Florida

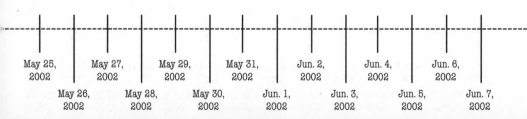

May 25, 2002	May 27, 2002	May 29, 2002	May 31, 2002	Jun. 2, 2002	Jun. 4, 2002	Jun. 6, 2002	
	May 26, 2002	May 28, 2002	May 30, 2002	Jun. 1, 2002	Jun. 3, 2002	Jun. 5, 2002	Jun. 7, 2002

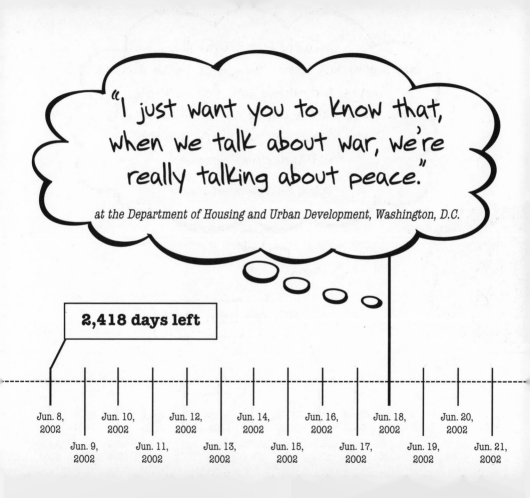

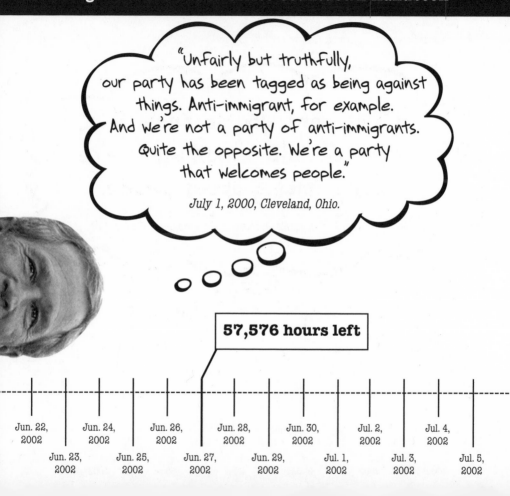

"Unfairly but truthfully, our party has been tagged as being against things. Anti-immigrant, for example. And we're not a party of anti-immigrants. Quite the opposite. We're a party that welcomes people."

July 1, 2000, Cleveland, Ohio.

57,576 hours left

Jun. 22, 2002

Jun. 23, 2002

Jun. 24, 2002

Jun. 25, 2002

Jun. 26, 2002

Jun. 27, 2002

Jun. 28, 2002

Jun. 29, 2002

Jun. 30, 2002

Jul. 1, 2002

Jul. 2, 2002

Jul. 3, 2002

Jul. 4, 2002

Jul. 5, 2002

"Our country puts $1 billion a year up to help feed the hungry. And we're by far the most generous nation in the world when it comes to that, and I'm proud to report that. This isn't a contest of who's the most generous. I'm just telling you as an aside. We're generous. We shouldn't be bragging about it. But we are. We're very generous."

July 16, 2003, Washington, D.C.

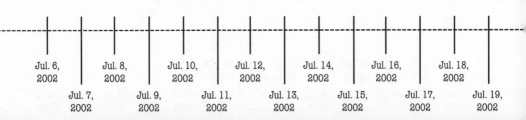

Jul. 6, 2002 — Jul. 7, 2002 — Jul. 8, 2002 — Jul. 9, 2002 — Jul. 10, 2002 — Jul. 11, 2002 — Jul. 12, 2002 — Jul. 13, 2002 — Jul. 14, 2002 — Jul. 15, 2002 — Jul. 16, 2002 — Jul. 17, 2002 — Jul. 18, 2002 — Jul. 19, 2002

"We ought to make the pie higher."

February 15, 2000, South Carolina debate

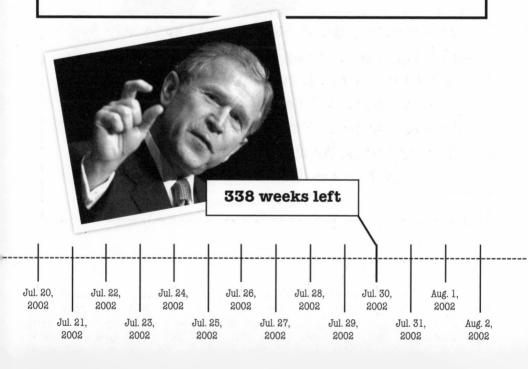

338 weeks left

Jul. 20,
2002

Jul. 21,
2002

Jul. 22,
2002

Jul. 23,
2002

Jul. 24,
2002

Jul. 25,
2002

Jul. 26,
2002

Jul. 27,
2002

Jul. 28,
2002

Jul. 29,
2002

Jul. 30,
2002

Jul. 31,
2002

Aug. 1,
2002

Aug. 2,
2002

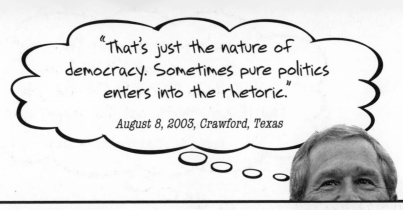

"That's just the nature of democracy. Sometimes pure politics enters into the rhetoric."

August 8, 2003, Crawford, Texas

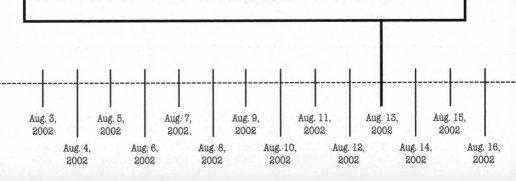

"The trial lawyers are very politically powerful... but here in Texas, we took them on and got some good medical—medical malpractice."

Waco, Texas

Aug. 3, 2002
Aug. 4, 2002
Aug. 5, 2002
Aug. 6, 2002
Aug. 7, 2002
Aug. 8, 2002
Aug. 9, 2002
Aug. 10, 2002
Aug. 11, 2002
Aug. 12, 2002
Aug. 13, 2002
Aug. 14, 2002
Aug. 15, 2002
Aug. 16, 2002

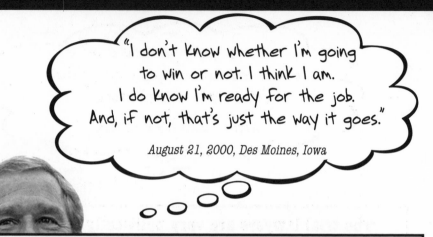

"I don't know whether I'm going to win or not. I think I am. I do know I'm ready for the job. And, if not, that's just the way it goes."

August 21, 2000, Des Moines, Iowa

"See, we love—we love freedom. That's what they didn't understand. They hate things; we love things. They act out of hatred; we don't seek revenge, we seek justice out of love."

Oklahoma City, Oklahoma

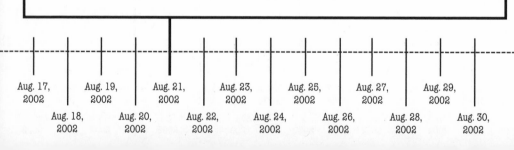

Aug. 17, 2002
Aug. 18, 2002
Aug. 19, 2002
Aug. 20, 2002
Aug. 21, 2002
Aug. 22, 2002
Aug. 23, 2002
Aug. 24, 2002
Aug. 25, 2002
Aug. 26, 2002
Aug. 27, 2002
Aug. 28, 2002
Aug. 29, 2002
Aug. 30, 2002

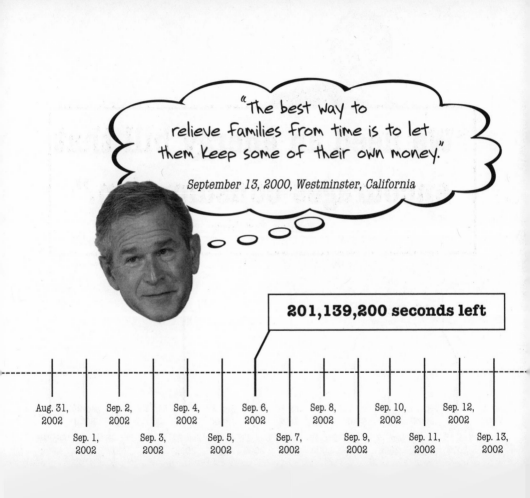

"We need an energy bill that encourages consumption."

Trenton, New Jersey

77.3 months left

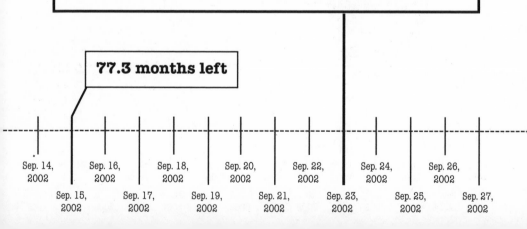

Sep. 14, 2002

Sep. 15, 2002

Sep. 16, 2002

Sep. 17, 2002

Sep. 18, 2002

Sep. 19, 2002

Sep. 20, 2002

Sep. 21, 2002

Sep. 22, 2002

Sep. 23, 2002

Sep. 24, 2002

Sep. 25, 2002

Sep. 26, 2002

Sep. 27, 2002

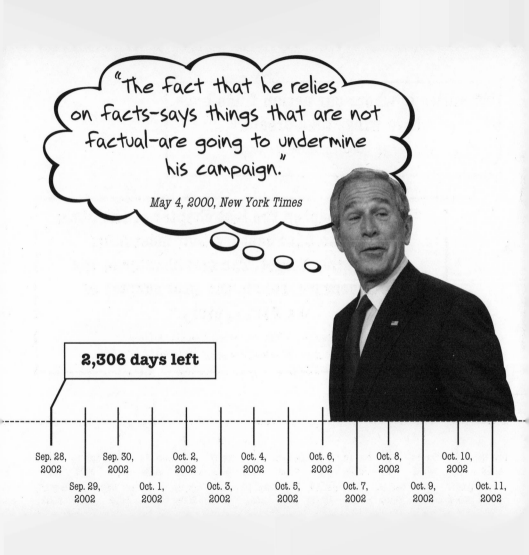

> **"Families is where our nation finds hope, where wings take dream."**
>
> *October 18, 2000, LaCrosse, Wisconsin*

> **"That's a chapter, the last chapter of the 20th, 20th, the 21st century that most of us would rather forget. The last chapter of the 20th century. This is the first chapter of the 21st century."**
>
> *October 24, 2000, Arlington Heights, Illinois, about the Monica Lewinsky controversy*

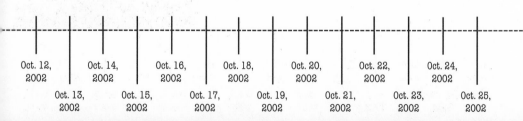

Oct. 12, 2002
Oct. 13, 2002
Oct. 14, 2002
Oct. 15, 2002
Oct. 16, 2002
Oct. 17, 2002
Oct. 18, 2002
Oct. 19, 2002
Oct. 20, 2002
Oct. 21, 2002
Oct. 22, 2002
Oct. 23, 2002
Oct. 24, 2002
Oct. 25, 2002

"I don't bring God into my life to—to, you know, kind of be a political person."

April 24, 2003, aboard Air Force One

3,274,560 minutes left

Oct. 26, 2002   Oct. 27, 2002   Oct. 28, 2002   Oct. 29, 2002   Oct. 30, 2002   Oct. 31, 2002   Nov. 1, 2002   Nov. 2, 2002   Nov. 3, 2002   Nov. 4, 2002   Nov. 5, 2002   Nov. 6, 2002   Nov. 7, 2002   Nov. 8, 2002

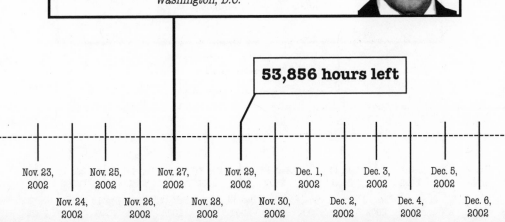

"The law I sign today directs new funds and new focus to the task of collecting vital intelligence on terrorist threats and on weapons of mass production."

Washington, D.C.

53,856 hours left

Nov. 23, 2002

Nov. 24, 2002

Nov. 25, 2002

Nov. 26, 2002

Nov. 27, 2002

Nov. 28, 2002

Nov. 29, 2002

Nov. 30, 2002

Dec. 1, 2002

Dec. 2, 2002

Dec. 3, 2002

Dec. 4, 2002

Dec. 5, 2002

Dec. 6, 2002

> "I mean, I read the newspaper.
> I mean, I can tell you what the headlines are.
> I must confess, if I think the story is, like,
> not a fair appraisal, I'll move on.
> But I know what the story's about."
>
> *December 12, 2005, Philadelphia, PA*

2,227 days left

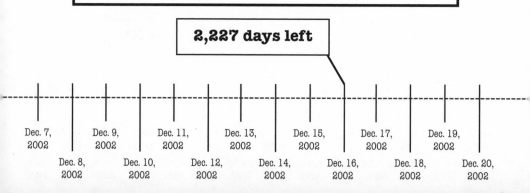

Dec. 7, 2002   Dec. 8, 2002   Dec. 9, 2002   Dec. 10, 2002   Dec. 11, 2002   Dec. 12, 2002   Dec. 13, 2002   Dec. 14, 2002   Dec. 15, 2002   Dec. 16, 2002   Dec. 17, 2002   Dec. 18, 2002   Dec. 19, 2002   Dec. 20, 2002

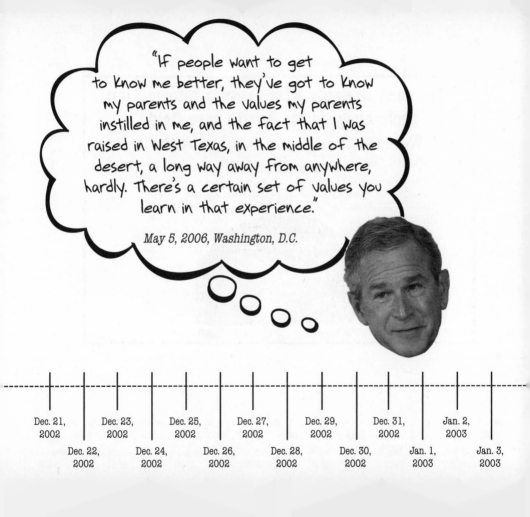

"We need to apply 21st-century information technology to the health care field. We need to have our medical records put on the I.T."

January 5, 2005, Collinsville, Illinois

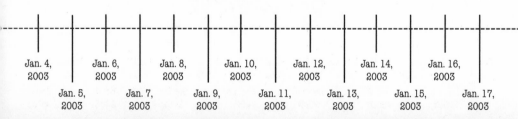

Jan. 4, 2003

Jan. 5, 2003

Jan. 6, 2003

Jan. 7, 2003

Jan. 8, 2003

Jan. 9, 2003

Jan. 10, 2003

Jan. 11, 2003

Jan. 12, 2003

Jan. 13, 2003

Jan. 14, 2003

Jan. 15, 2003

Jan. 16, 2003

Jan. 17, 2003

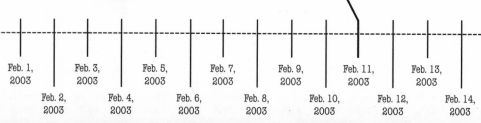

"Finally, the desk, where we'll have our picture taken in front of—is nine other Presidents used it. This was given to us by Queen Victoria in the 1870s, I think it was. President Roosevelt put the door in so people would not know he was in a wheelchair. John Kennedy put his head out the door."

May 5, 2006, The Oval Office

2,170 days left

Feb. 1, 2003

Feb. 2, 2003

Feb. 3, 2003

Feb. 4, 2003

Feb. 5, 2003

Feb. 6, 2003

Feb. 7, 2003

Feb. 8, 2003

Feb. 9, 2003

Feb. 10, 2003

Feb. 11, 2003

Feb. 12, 2003

Feb. 13, 2003

Feb. 14, 2003

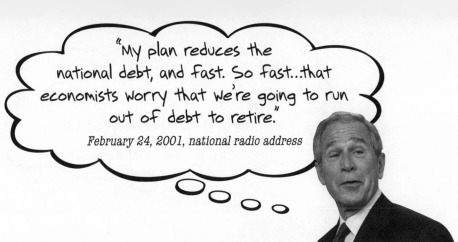

"My plan reduces the national debt, and fast. So fast...that economists worry that we're going to run out of debt to retire."

February 24, 2001, national radio address

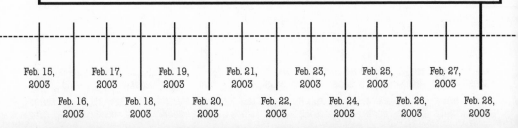

Former lobbyist and indicted embezzler Jack Abramoff's birthday.

"Can you smell money?!?!?!" —Jack Abramoff

Born on February 28, 1959

Feb. 15, 2003

Feb. 16, 2003

Feb. 17, 2003

Feb. 18, 2003

Feb. 19, 2003

Feb. 20, 2003

Feb. 21, 2003

Feb. 22, 2003

Feb. 23, 2003

Feb. 24, 2003

Feb. 25, 2003

Feb. 26, 2003

Feb. 27, 2003

Feb. 28, 2003

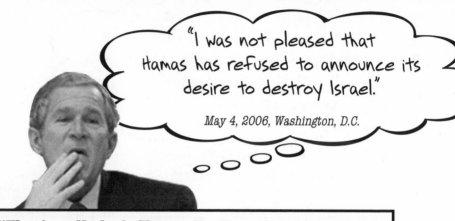

"I was not pleased that Hamas has refused to announce its desire to destroy Israel."

May 4, 2006, Washington, D.C.

"That's called, *A Charge To Keep*, based upon a religious hymn. The hymn talks about serving God. The president's job is never to promote a religion."

May 5, 2006, The Oval Office

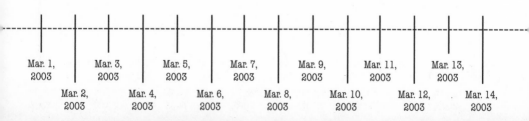

Mar. 1, 2003 Mar. 3, 2003 Mar. 5, 2003 Mar. 7, 2003 Mar. 9, 2003 Mar. 11, 2003 Mar. 13, 2003

Mar. 2, 2003 Mar. 4, 2003 Mar. 6, 2003 Mar. 8, 2003 Mar. 10, 2003 Mar. 12, 2003 Mar. 14, 2003

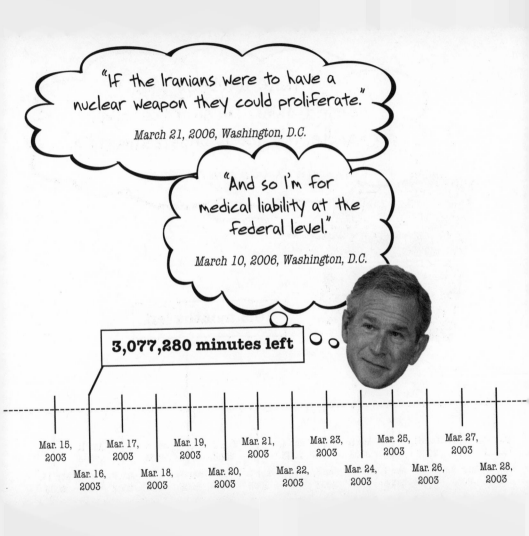

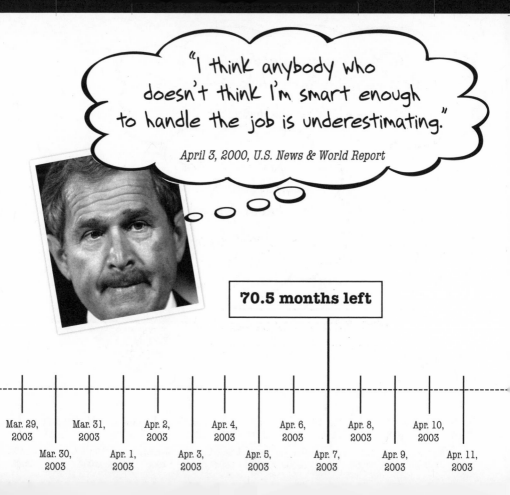

"This foreign policy stuff is a little frustrating."

April 23, 2002, The New York Daily News

"You're free. And freedom is beautiful.
And, you know, it will take time to restore chaos and
order—order out of chaos. But we will."

Washington, D.C

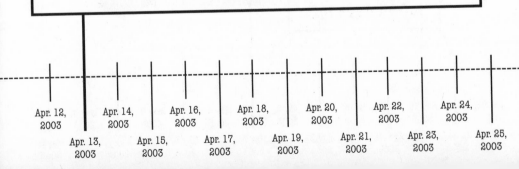

Apr. 12, 2003

Apr. 13, 2003

Apr. 14, 2003

Apr. 15, 2003

Apr. 16, 2003

Apr. 17, 2003

Apr. 18, 2003

Apr. 19, 2003

Apr. 20, 2003

Apr. 21, 2003

Apr. 22, 2003

Apr. 23, 2003

Apr. 24, 2003

Apr. 25, 2003

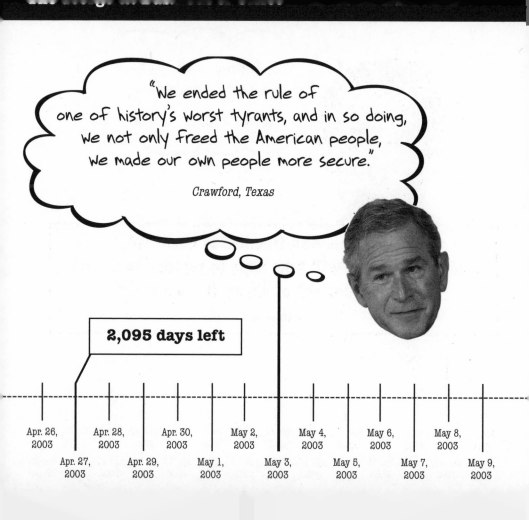

**"First, let me make it very clear:
poor people aren't necessarily killers.
Just because you happen to be not rich doesn't
mean you're willing to kill."**

Washington, D.C.

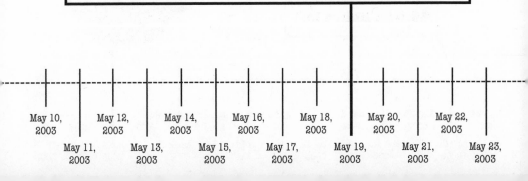

May 10, 2003

May 11, 2003

May 12, 2003

May 13, 2003

May 14, 2003

May 15, 2003

May 16, 2003

May 17, 2003

May 18, 2003

May 19, 2003

May 20, 2003

May 21, 2003

May 22, 2003

May 23, 2003

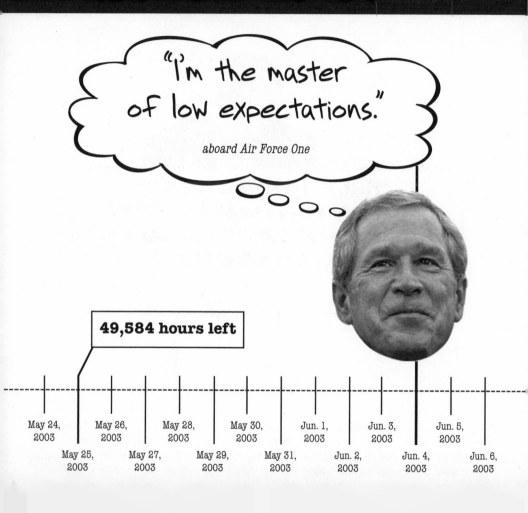

"I'm the master of low expectations."

aboard Air Force One

49,584 hours left

May 24, 2003 | May 26, 2003 | May 28, 2003 | May 30, 2003 | Jun. 1, 2003 | Jun. 3, 2003 | Jun. 5, 2003

May 25, 2003 | May 27, 2003 | May 29, 2003 | May 31, 2003 | Jun. 2, 2003 | Jun. 4, 2003 | Jun. 6, 2003

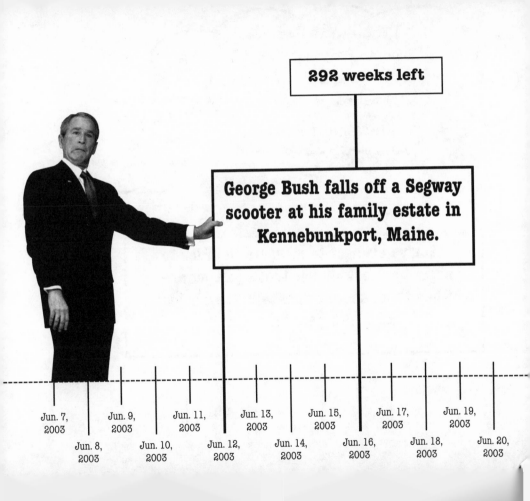

292 weeks left

George Bush falls off a Segway scooter at his family estate in Kennebunkport, Maine.

Jun. 7, 2003
Jun. 8, 2003
Jun. 9, 2003
Jun. 10, 2003
Jun. 11, 2003
Jun. 12, 2003
Jun. 13, 2003
Jun. 14, 2003
Jun. 15, 2003
Jun. 16, 2003
Jun. 17, 2003
Jun. 18, 2003
Jun. 19, 2003
Jun. 20, 2003

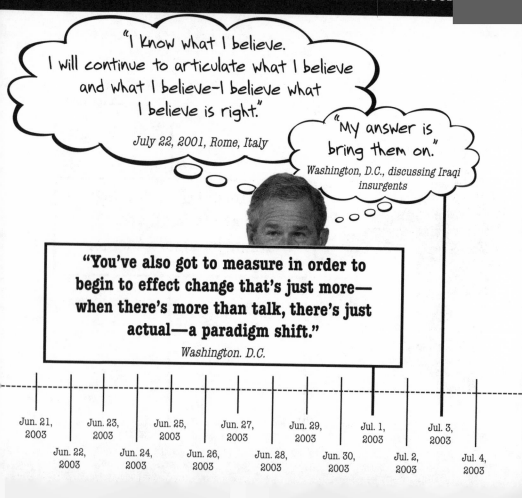

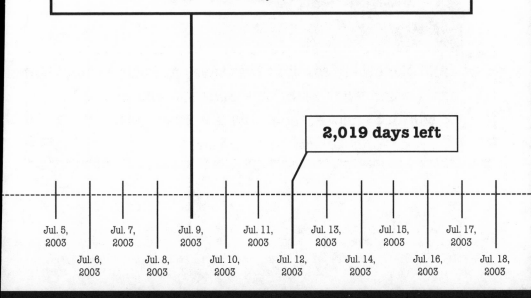

"I believe what I said yesterday.
I don't know what I said, but I know what I think,
and, well, I assume it's what I said."
—Donald Rumsfeld

Secretary of Defense Donald Rumsfeld's birthday
Born on July 9, 1932

2,019 days left

Jul. 5, 2003
Jul. 6, 2003
Jul. 7, 2003
Jul. 8, 2003
Jul. 9, 2003
Jul. 10, 2003
Jul. 11, 2003
Jul. 12, 2003
Jul. 13, 2003
Jul. 14, 2003
Jul. 15, 2003
Jul. 16, 2003
Jul. 17, 2003
Jul. 18, 2003

"We had a good Cabinet meeting, talked about a lot of issues. Secretary of State and Defense brought us up to date about our desires to spread freedom and peace around the world."

Washington, D.C.

"And the other lesson is that there are people who can't stand what America stands for, and desire to conflict great harm on the American people."

Pittsburgh, Pennsylvania

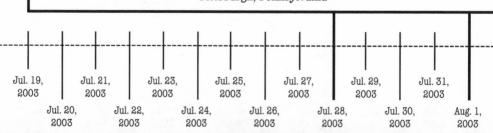

Jul. 19, 2003	Jul. 21, 2003	Jul. 23, 2003	Jul. 25, 2003	Jul. 27, 2003	Jul. 29, 2003	Jul. 31, 2003
Jul. 20, 2003	Jul. 22, 2003	Jul. 24, 2003	Jul. 26, 2003	Jul. 28, 2003	Jul. 30, 2003	Aug. 1, 2003

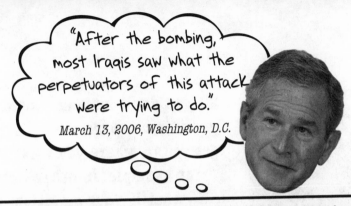

"After the bombing, most Iraqis saw what the perpetuators of this attack were trying to do."

March 13, 2006, Washington, D.C.

"I believe that a prosperous, democratic Pakistan will be a steadfast partner for America, a peaceful neighbor for India, and a force for freedom and moderation in the Arab world."

March 3, 2006, Islamabad, Pakistan (which is not an Arab country)

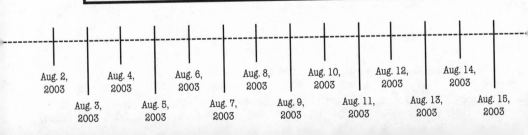

Aug. 2, 2003
Aug. 3, 2003
Aug. 4, 2003
Aug. 5, 2003
Aug. 6, 2003
Aug. 7, 2003
Aug. 8, 2003
Aug. 9, 2003
Aug. 10, 2003
Aug. 11, 2003
Aug. 12, 2003
Aug. 13, 2003
Aug. 14, 2003
Aug. 15, 2003

"If you don't have any ambitions,
the minimum-wage job isn't going to
get you to where you want to get,
for example. In other words,
what is your ambitions?
And oh, by the way, if that is
your ambition, here's what it's
going to take to achieve it."

August 29, 2002, Little Rock, Arkansas

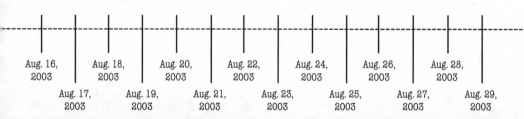

Aug. 16, 2003 Aug. 18, 2003 Aug. 20, 2003 Aug. 22, 2003 Aug. 24, 2003 Aug. 26, 2003 Aug. 28, 2003

Aug. 17, 2003 Aug. 19, 2003 Aug. 21, 2003 Aug. 23, 2003 Aug. 25, 2003 Aug. 27, 2003 Aug. 29, 2003

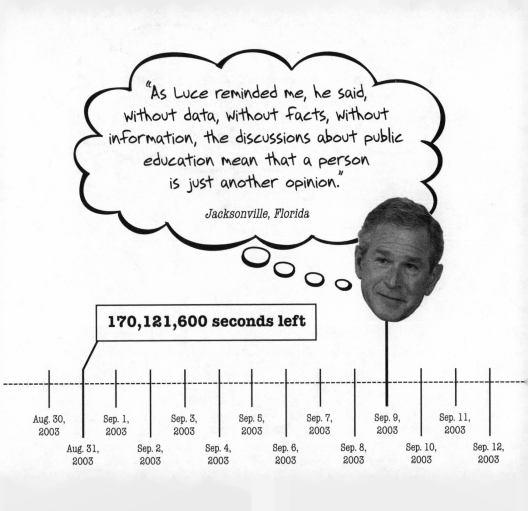

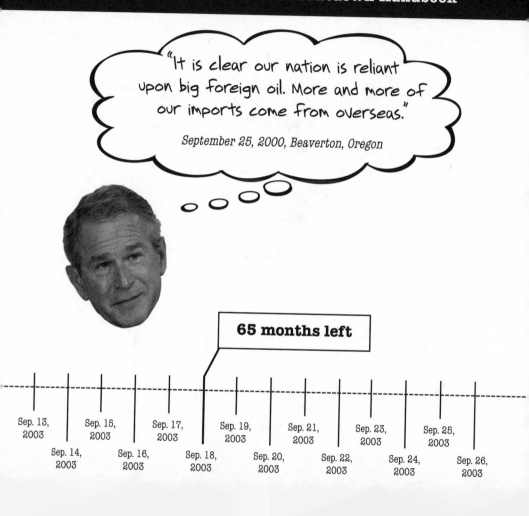

"It is clear our nation is reliant upon big foreign oil. More and more of our imports come from overseas."

September 25, 2000, Beaverton, Oregon

65 months left

Sep. 13, 2003
Sep. 14, 2003
Sep. 15, 2003
Sep. 16, 2003
Sep. 17, 2003
Sep. 18, 2003
Sep. 19, 2003
Sep. 20, 2003
Sep. 21, 2003
Sep. 22, 2003
Sep. 23, 2003
Sep. 24, 2003
Sep. 25, 2003
Sep. 26, 2003

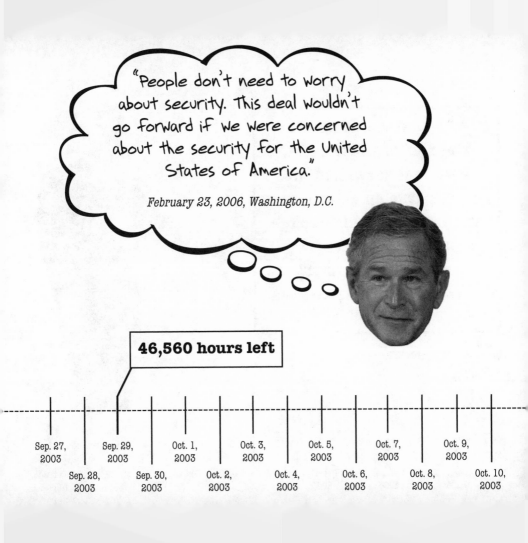

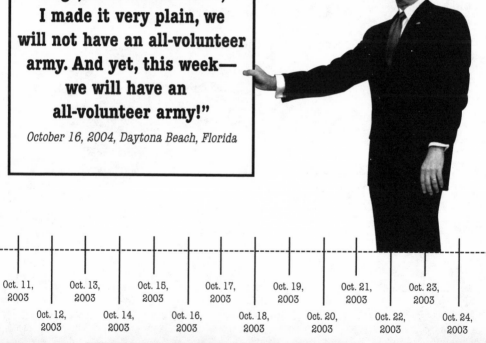

"After standing on the stage, after the debates, I made it very plain, we will not have an all-volunteer army. And yet, this week— we will have an all-volunteer army!"

October 16, 2004, Daytona Beach, Florida

Oct. 11, 2003

Oct. 12, 2003

Oct. 13, 2003

Oct. 14, 2003

Oct. 15, 2003

Oct. 16, 2003

Oct. 17, 2003

Oct. 18, 2003

Oct. 19, 2003

Oct. 20, 2003

Oct. 21, 2003

Oct. 22, 2003

Oct. 23, 2003

Oct. 24, 2003

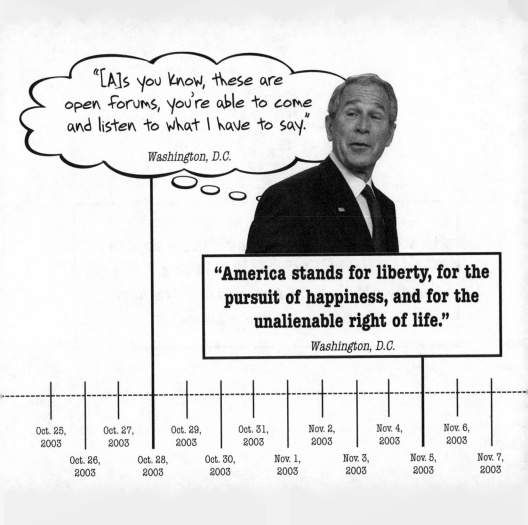

"And I want those who are questioning it to step up and explain why all of a sudden a Middle Eastern company is held to a different standard than a Great British company."

February 21, 2006, Air Force One

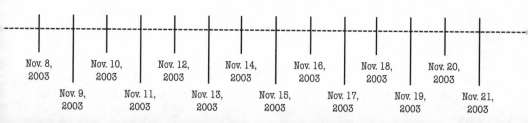

Nov. 8, 2003

Nov. 9, 2003

Nov. 10, 2003

Nov. 11, 2003

Nov. 12, 2003

Nov. 13, 2003

Nov. 14, 2003

Nov. 15, 2003

Nov. 16, 2003

Nov. 17, 2003

Nov. 18, 2003

Nov. 19, 2003

Nov. 20, 2003

Nov. 21, 2003

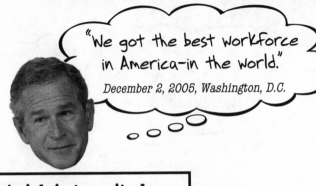

"We got the best workforce in America–in the world."

December 2, 2005, Washington, D.C.

"The legislature's job is to write law. It's the executive branch's job to interpret law."

November 22, 2000, Austin, Texas

1,875 days left

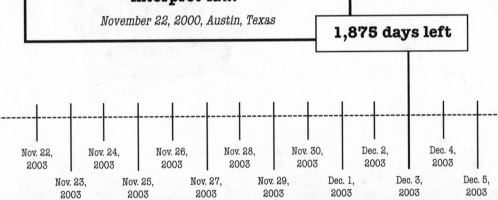

Nov. 22, 2003

Nov. 23, 2003

Nov. 24, 2003

Nov. 25, 2003

Nov. 26, 2003

Nov. 27, 2003

Nov. 28, 2003

Nov. 29, 2003

Nov. 30, 2003

Dec. 1, 2003

Dec. 2, 2003

Dec. 3, 2003

Dec. 4, 2003

Dec. 5, 2003

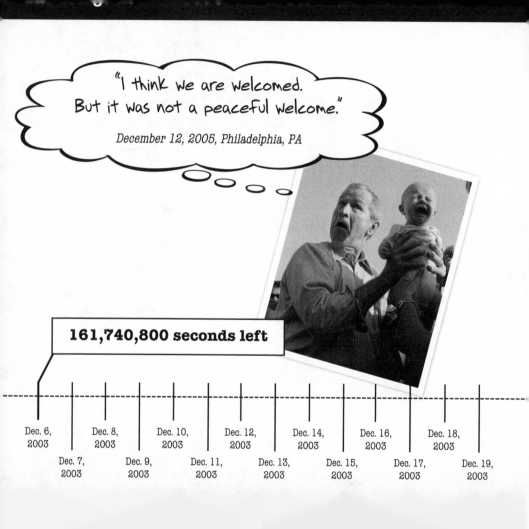

"I'm going to work with every Cabinet member to set a series of goals for each Cabinet."

January 2, 2001, Austin, Texas

Dec. 20, 2003

Dec. 21, 2003

Dec. 22, 2003

Dec. 23, 2003

Dec. 24, 2003

Dec. 25, 2003

Dec. 26, 2003

Dec. 27, 2003

Dec. 28, 2003

Dec. 29, 2003

Dec. 30, 2003

Dec. 31, 2003

Jan. 1, 2004

Jan. 2, 2004

"I want to thank the astronauts who are with us, the courageous spacial entrepreneurs who set such a wonderful example for the young of our country."

Washington, D.C.

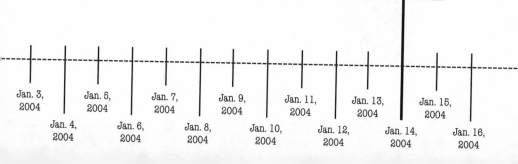

Jan. 3, 2004

Jan. 4, 2004

Jan. 5, 2004

Jan. 6, 2004

Jan. 7, 2004

Jan. 8, 2004

Jan. 9, 2004

Jan. 10, 2004

Jan. 11, 2004

Jan. 12, 2004

Jan. 13, 2004

Jan. 14, 2004

Jan. 15, 2004

Jan. 16, 2004

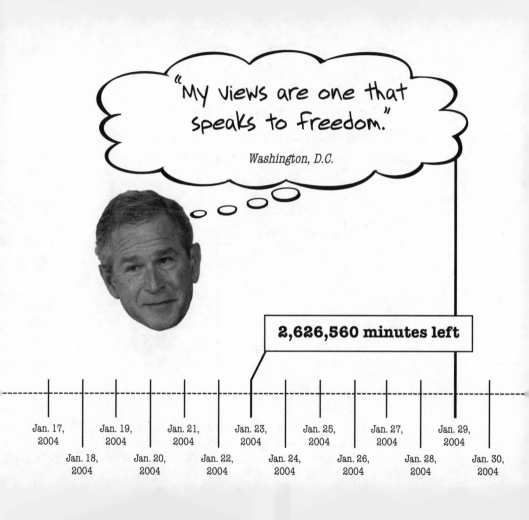

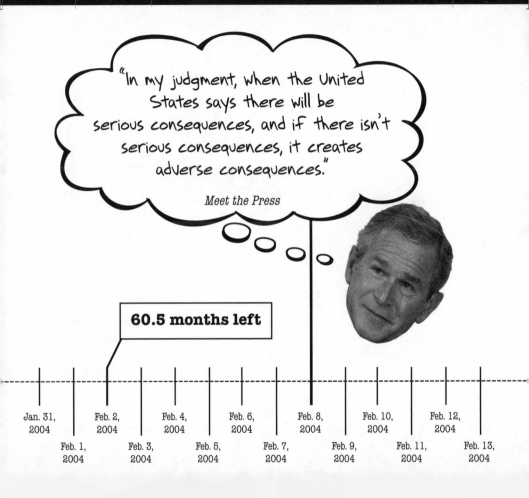

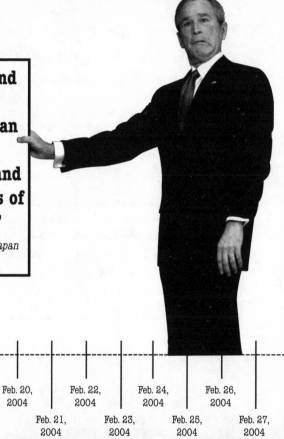

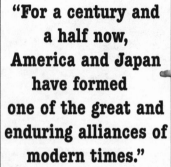

"For a century and a half now, America and Japan have formed one of the great and enduring alliances of modern times."

February 18, 2002, Tokyo, Japan

Feb. 14, 2004

Feb. 15, 2004

Feb. 16, 2004

Feb. 17, 2004

Feb. 18, 2004

Feb. 19, 2004

Feb. 20, 2004

Feb. 21, 2004

Feb. 22, 2004

Feb. 23, 2004

Feb. 24, 2004

Feb. 25, 2004

Feb. 26, 2004

Feb. 27, 2004

> "He's kind of a-probably feeling his oats pretty good about that time."
>
> *At the Faith-Based and Community Initiatives Conference, describing when Rabbi Borovitz met his wife, Harriet*

> **"The march to war hurt the economy. Laura reminded me a while ago that remember what was on the TV screens—she calls me, 'George W.'—'George W.' I call her, 'First Lady.' No, anyway— she said, we said, march to war on our TV screen."**
>
> *Bay Shore, New York*

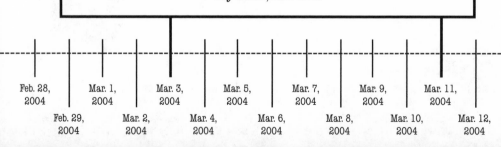

Feb. 28, 2004	Mar. 1, 2004	Mar. 3, 2004	Mar. 5, 2004	Mar. 7, 2004	Mar. 9, 2004	Mar. 11, 2004
Feb. 29, 2004	Mar. 2, 2004	Mar. 4, 2004	Mar. 6, 2004	Mar. 8, 2004	Mar. 10, 2004	Mar. 12, 2004

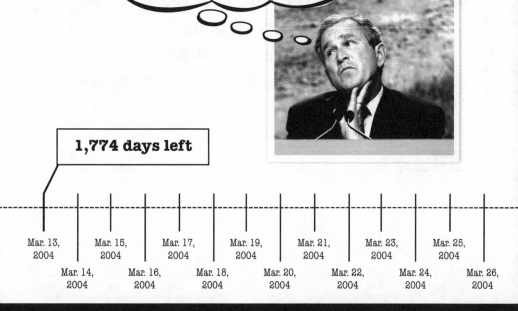

"Those weapons of mass destruction have got to be here somewhere."

March 28, 2004, The Radio & Television Correspondents' Dinner, captioning a photo of himself looking under his desk

1,774 days left

Mar. 13, 2004
Mar. 14, 2004
Mar. 15, 2004
Mar. 16, 2004
Mar. 17, 2004
Mar. 18, 2004
Mar. 19, 2004
Mar. 20, 2004
Mar. 21, 2004
Mar. 22, 2004
Mar. 23, 2004
Mar. 24, 2004
Mar. 25, 2004
Mar. 26, 2004

"I think it's really important for this great state of baseball to reach out to people of all walks of life to make sure that the sport is inclusive. The best way to do it is to convince little kids how to— the beauty of playing baseball."

February 13, 2006, Washington, D.C.

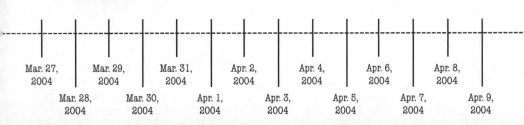

Mar. 27, 2004 Mar. 28, 2004 Mar. 29, 2004 Mar. 30, 2004 Mar. 31, 2004 Apr. 1, 2004 Apr. 2, 2004 Apr. 3, 2004 Apr. 4, 2004 Apr. 5, 2004 Apr. 6, 2004 Apr. 7, 2004 Apr. 8, 2004 Apr. 9, 2004

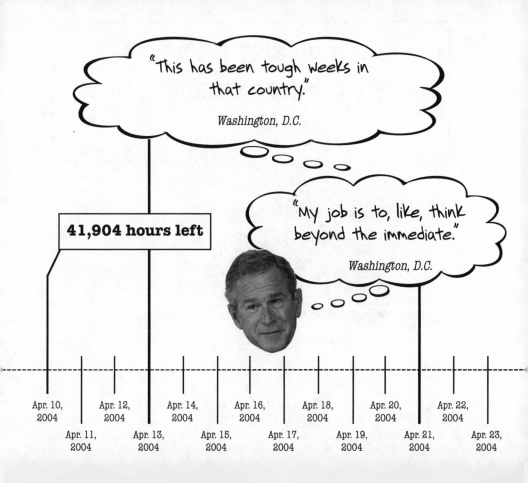

> # "It's clearly a budget.
> # It's got a lot of numbers in it."
>
> *May 5, 2000, Reuters*

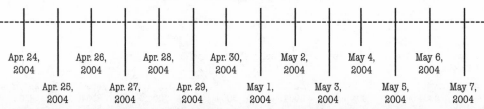

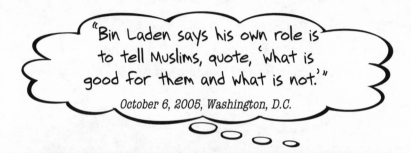

"Bin Laden says his own role is to tell Muslims, quote, 'what is good for them and what is not.'"

October 6, 2005, Washington, D.C.

"I mean, there was a pretty serious international effort to say to Saddam Hussein, you're a threat. And the 9/11 attacks extenuated that threat, as far as I—concerned."

December 12, 2005, Philadelphia, Pennsylvania

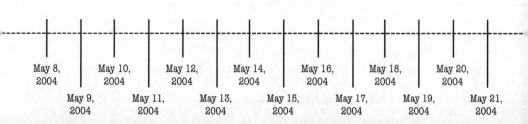

May 8, 2004

May 9, 2004

May 10, 2004

May 11, 2004

May 12, 2004

May 13, 2004

May 14, 2004

May 15, 2004

May 16, 2004

May 17, 2004

May 18, 2004

May 19, 2004

May 20, 2004

May 21, 2004

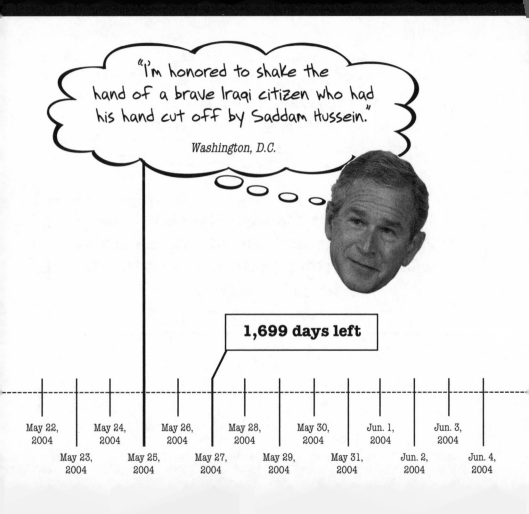

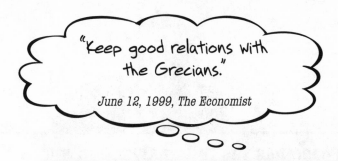

"Keep good relations with the Grecians."

June 12, 1999, The Economist

"Russia is no longer our enemy and therefore we shouldn't be locked into a Cold War mentality that says we keep the peace by blowing each other up. In my attitude, that's old, that's tired, that's stale."

June 8, 2001, Des Moines, Iowa

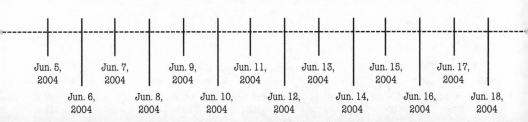

> **"This case has the full analyzation and has been looked at a lot. I understand the emotionality of death penalty cases."**
>
> *June 23, 2000, Seattle Post-Intelligencer*

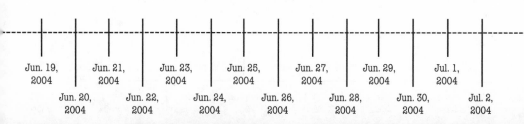

Jun. 19, 2004   Jun. 21, 2004   Jun. 23, 2004   Jun. 25, 2004   Jun. 27, 2004   Jun. 29, 2004   Jul. 1, 2004

Jun. 20, 2004   Jun. 22, 2004   Jun. 24, 2004   Jun. 26, 2004   Jun. 28, 2004   Jun. 30, 2004   Jul. 2, 2004

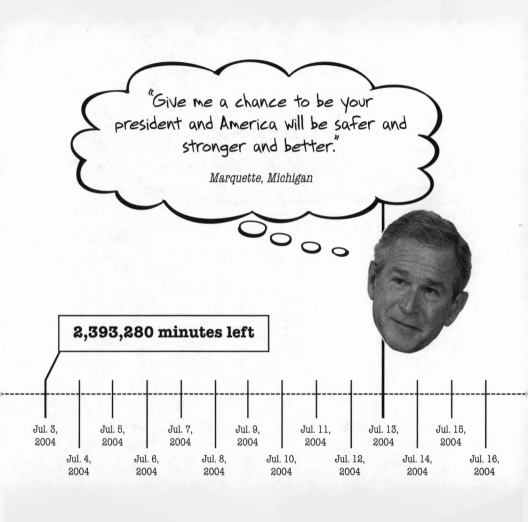

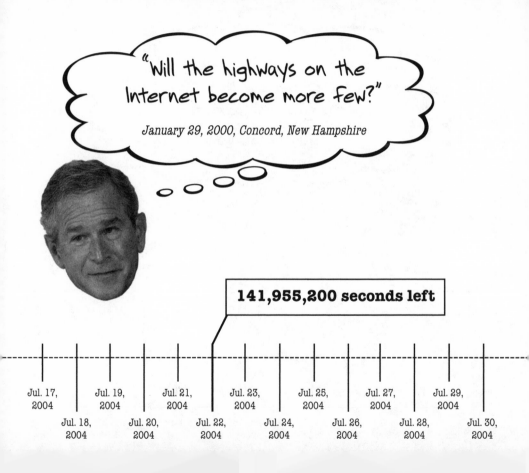

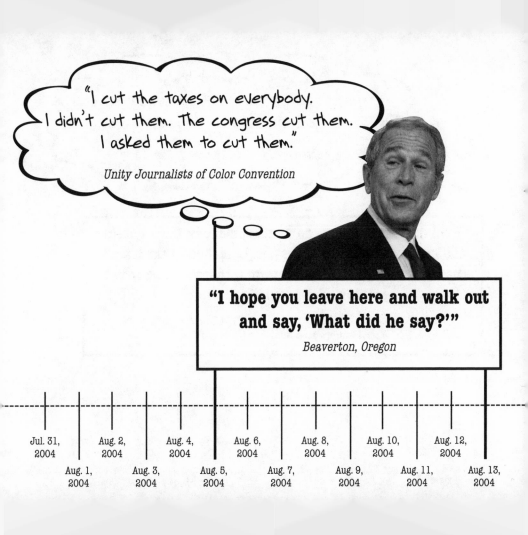

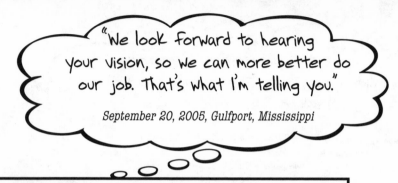

"We look forward to hearing your vision, so we can more better do our job. That's what I'm telling you."

September 20, 2005, Gulfport, Mississippi

"I think it's important to bring somebody from outside the system, the judicial system, somebody that hasn't been on the bench and, therefore, there's not a lot of opinions for people to look at."

October 4, 2005, Washington, D.C., justifying his nomination of Harriet Miers as a Supreme Court Justice.

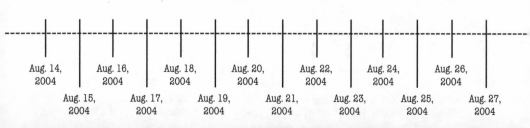

Aug. 14, 2004

Aug. 15, 2004

Aug. 16, 2004

Aug. 17, 2004

Aug. 18, 2004

Aug. 19, 2004

Aug. 20, 2004

Aug. 21, 2004

Aug. 22, 2004

Aug. 23, 2004

Aug. 24, 2004

Aug. 25, 2004

Aug. 26, 2004

Aug. 27, 2004

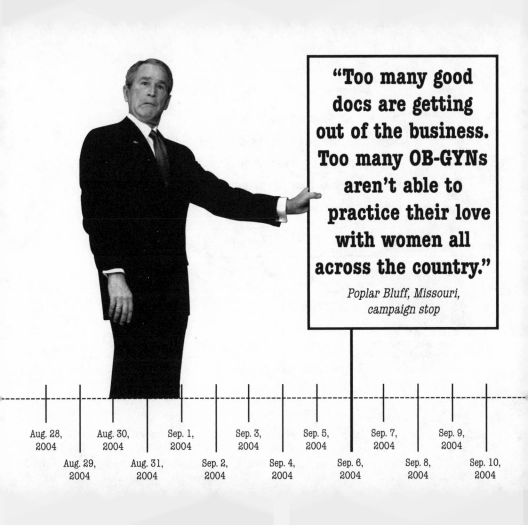

"Too many good docs are getting out of the business. Too many OB-GYNs aren't able to practice their love with women all across the country."

Poplar Bluff, Missouri, campaign stop

Aug. 28, 2004
Aug. 29, 2004
Aug. 30, 2004
Aug. 31, 2004
Sep. 1, 2004
Sep. 2, 2004
Sep. 3, 2004
Sep. 4, 2004
Sep. 5, 2004
Sep. 6, 2004
Sep. 7, 2004
Sep. 8, 2004
Sep. 9, 2004
Sep. 10, 2004

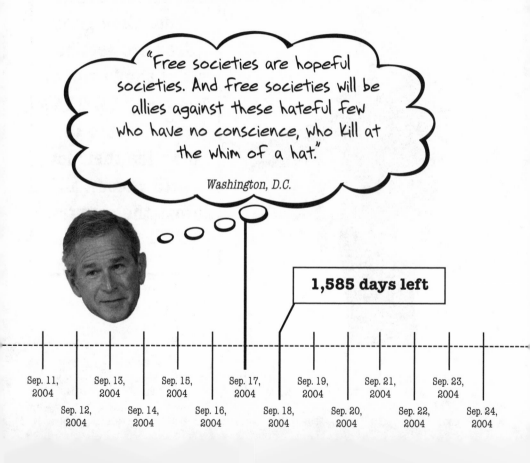

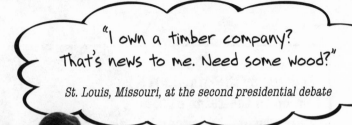

"I own a timber company?
That's news to me. Need some wood?"

St. Louis, Missouri, at the second presidential debate

"The enemy understands a free Iraq will be a
major defeat in their ideology of hatred.
That's why they're fighting so vociferously."

Coral Gables, Florida

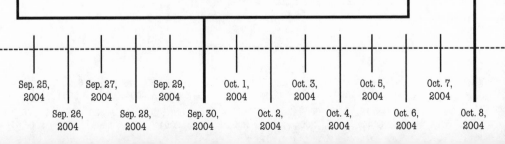

Sep. 25, 2004

Sep. 26, 2004

Sep. 27, 2004

Sep. 28, 2004

Sep. 29, 2004

Sep. 30, 2004

Oct. 1, 2004

Oct. 2, 2004

Oct. 3, 2004

Oct. 4, 2004

Oct. 5, 2004

Oct. 6, 2004

Oct. 7, 2004

Oct. 8, 2004

"September the 4th, 2001, I stood in the ruins of the Twin Towers. It's a day I will never forget."

Marlton, New Jersey

37,512 hours left

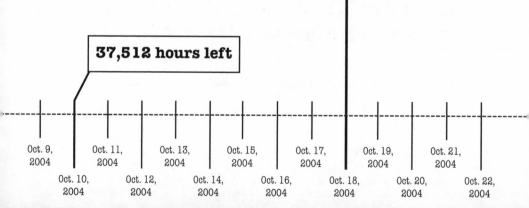

Oct. 9, 2004

Oct. 10, 2004

Oct. 11, 2004

Oct. 12, 2004

Oct. 13, 2004

Oct. 14, 2004

Oct. 15, 2004

Oct. 16, 2004

Oct. 17, 2004

Oct. 18, 2004

Oct. 19, 2004

Oct. 20, 2004

Oct. 21, 2004

Oct. 22, 2004

"...Out of the rubble of Trent Lott's house—he's lost his entire house—there's going to be a fantastic house. And I'm looking forward to sitting on the porch."

September 2, 2005, Mobile, Alabama, surveying the damage wrought by Hurricane Katrina in the area

"**So please give cash money to organizations that are directly involved in helping save lives—save the life who had been affected by Hurricane Katrina.**"

September 6, 2005, Washington, D.C.

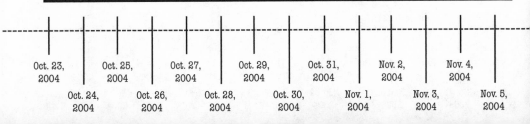

| Oct. 23, 2004 | Oct. 25, 2004 | Oct. 27, 2004 | Oct. 29, 2004 | Oct. 31, 2004 | Nov. 2, 2004 | Nov. 4, 2004 |
| Oct. 24, 2004 | Oct. 26, 2004 | Oct. 28, 2004 | Oct. 30, 2004 | Nov. 1, 2004 | Nov. 3, 2004 | Nov. 5, 2004 |

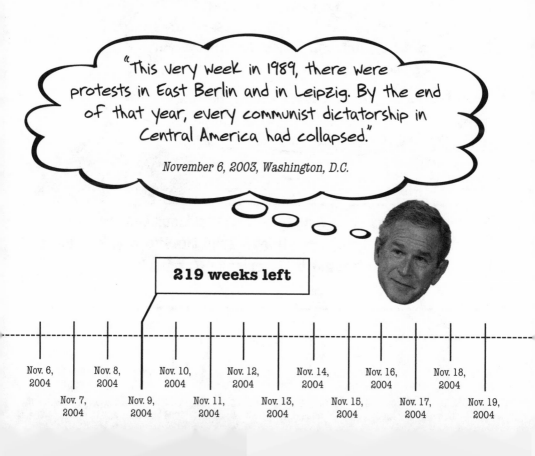

"As far as the legal hassling and wrangling and posturing in Florida, I would suggest you talk to our team in Florida led by Jim Baker."

November 30, 2000, Crawford, Texas

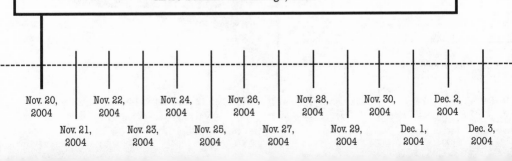

"We thought we were protected forever from trade policy or terrorist attacks because oceans protected us."

APEC Summit in Santiago, Chile

Nov. 20, 2004

Nov. 21, 2004

Nov. 22, 2004

Nov. 23, 2004

Nov. 24, 2004

Nov. 25, 2004

Nov. 26, 2004

Nov. 27, 2004

Nov. 28, 2004

Nov. 29, 2004

Nov. 30, 2004

Dec. 1, 2004

Dec. 2, 2004

Dec. 3, 2004

"And so during these holiday seasons, we thank our blessings..."

Fort Belvoir, Virginia

Dec. 4, 2004
Dec. 5, 2004
Dec. 6, 2004
Dec. 7, 2004
Dec. 8, 2004
Dec. 9, 2004
Dec. 10, 2004
Dec. 11, 2004
Dec. 12, 2004
Dec. 13, 2004
Dec. 14, 2004
Dec. 15, 2004
Dec. 16, 2004
Dec. 17, 2004

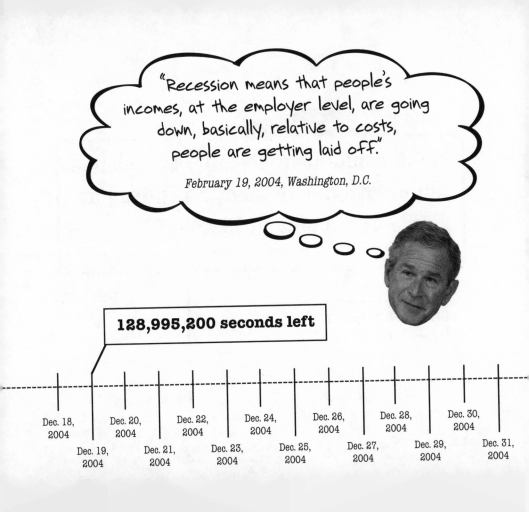

"Who could have possibly envisioned an erection—an election in Iraq at this point in history?"

White House speech

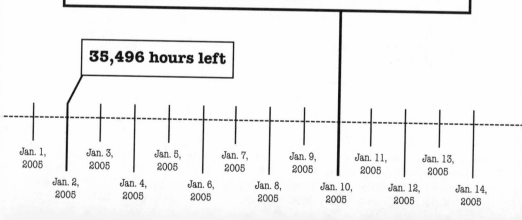

35,496 hours left

Jan. 1, 2005

Jan. 2, 2005

Jan. 3, 2005

Jan. 4, 2005

Jan. 5, 2005

Jan. 6, 2005

Jan. 7, 2005

Jan. 8, 2005

Jan. 9, 2005

Jan. 10, 2005

Jan. 11, 2005

Jan. 12, 2005

Jan. 13, 2005

Jan. 14, 2005

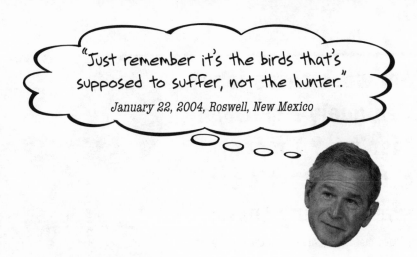

"Just remember it's the birds that's supposed to suffer, not the hunter."

January 22, 2004, Roswell, New Mexico

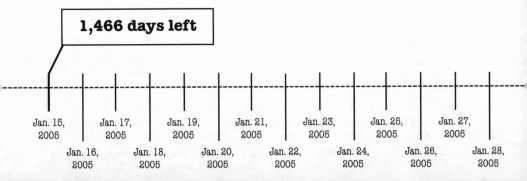

1,466 days left

Jan. 15, 2005   Jan. 17, 2005   Jan. 19, 2005   Jan. 21, 2005   Jan. 23, 2005   Jan. 25, 2005   Jan. 27, 2005

Jan. 16, 2005   Jan. 18, 2005   Jan. 20, 2005   Jan. 22, 2005   Jan. 24, 2005   Jan. 26, 2005   Jan. 28, 2005

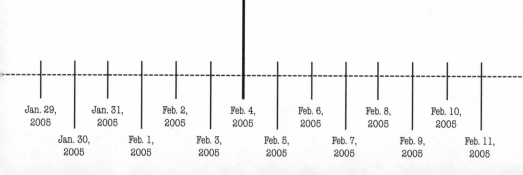

"You work three jobs? …Uniquely American, isn't it? I mean, that is fantastic that you're doing that."

to a divorced mother of three from Omaha, Nebraska

Jan. 29, 2005

Jan. 30, 2005

Jan. 31, 2005

Feb. 1, 2005

Feb. 2, 2005

Feb. 3, 2005

Feb. 4, 2005

Feb. 5, 2005

Feb. 6, 2005

Feb. 7, 2005

Feb. 8, 2005

Feb. 9, 2005

Feb. 10, 2005

Feb. 11, 2005

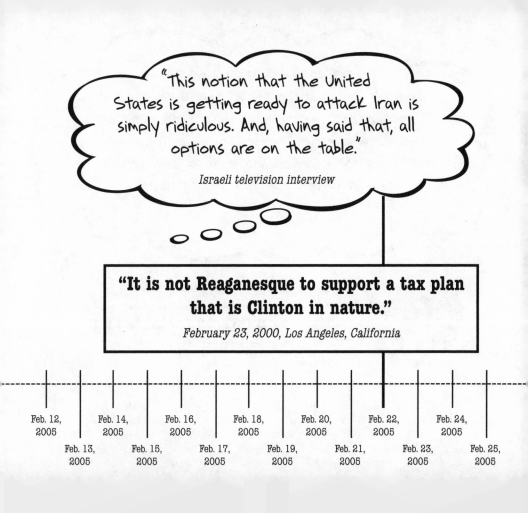

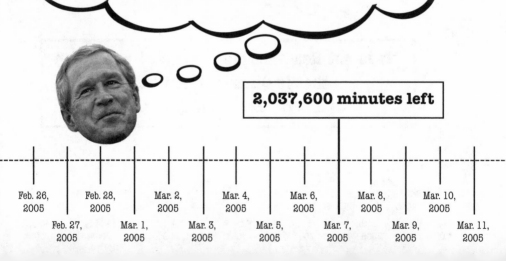

"I repeat: personal accounts do not permanently fix the solution."

Washington, D.C.

Mar. 12, 2005

Mar. 13, 2005

Mar. 14, 2005

Mar. 15, 2005

Mar. 16, 2005

Mar. 17, 2005

Mar. 18, 2005

Mar. 19, 2005

Mar. 20, 2005

Mar. 21, 2005

Mar. 22, 2005

Mar. 23, 2005

Mar. 24, 2005

Mar. 25, 2005

> ## "I urge all those who honor Terri Schiavo to continue to work to build a culture of life."
>
> *Offering his condolences to Terri Schiavo's family*

33,336 hours left

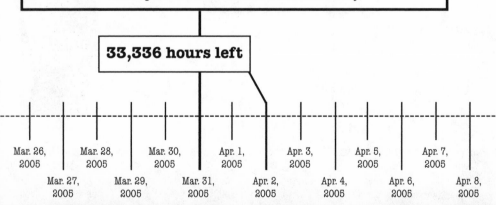

| Mar. 26, 2005 | Mar. 28, 2005 | Mar. 30, 2005 | Apr. 1, 2005 | Apr. 3, 2005 | Apr. 5, 2005 | Apr. 7, 2005 |
| Mar. 27, 2005 | Mar. 29, 2005 | Mar. 31, 2005 | Apr. 2, 2005 | Apr. 4, 2005 | Apr. 6, 2005 | Apr. 8, 2005 |

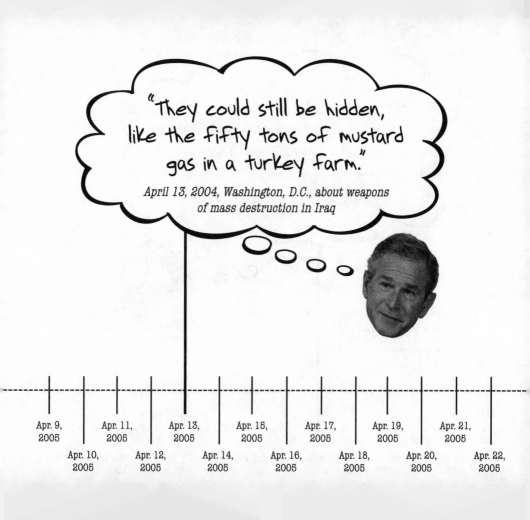

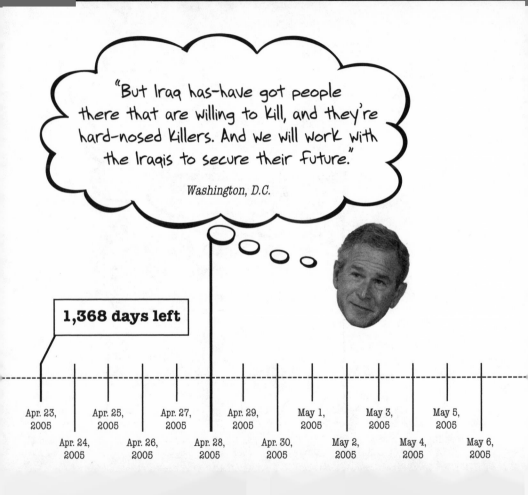

"But Iraq has–have got people there that are willing to kill, and they're hard-nosed killers. And we will work with the Iraqis to secure their future."

Washington, D.C.

1,368 days left

Apr. 23, 2005
Apr. 24, 2005
Apr. 25, 2005
Apr. 26, 2005
Apr. 27, 2005
Apr. 28, 2005
Apr. 29, 2005
Apr. 30, 2005
May 1, 2005
May 2, 2005
May 3, 2005
May 4, 2005
May 5, 2005
May 6, 2005

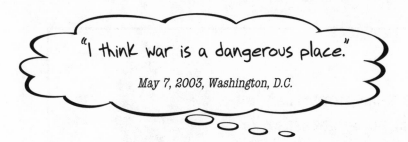

"I think war is a dangerous place."

May 7, 2003, Washington, D.C.

"For every fatal shooting, there were roughly three non-fatal shootings. And, folks, this is unacceptable in America...And we're going to do something about it."

May 14, 2001, Philadelphia, Pennsylvania

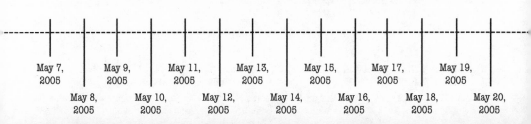

"The most important job is not to be governor, or first lady in my case."

January 30, 2000, San Antonio Express-News

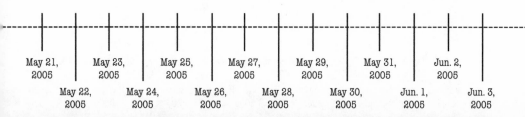

May 21, 2005

May 22, 2005

May 23, 2005

May 24, 2005

May 25, 2005

May 26, 2005

May 27, 2005

May 28, 2005

May 29, 2005

May 30, 2005

May 31, 2005

Jun. 1, 2005

Jun. 2, 2005

Jun. 3, 2005

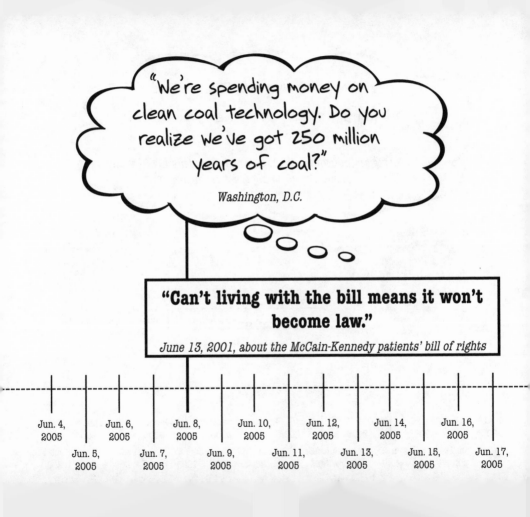

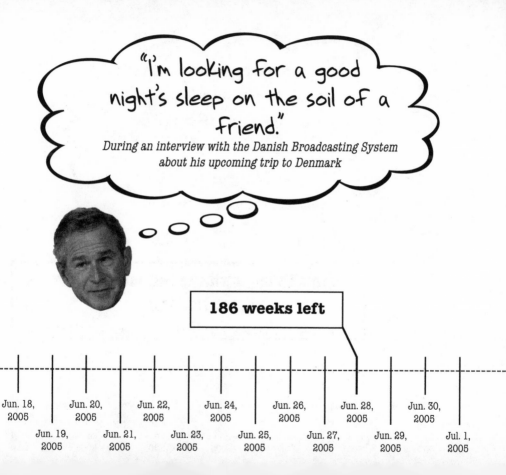

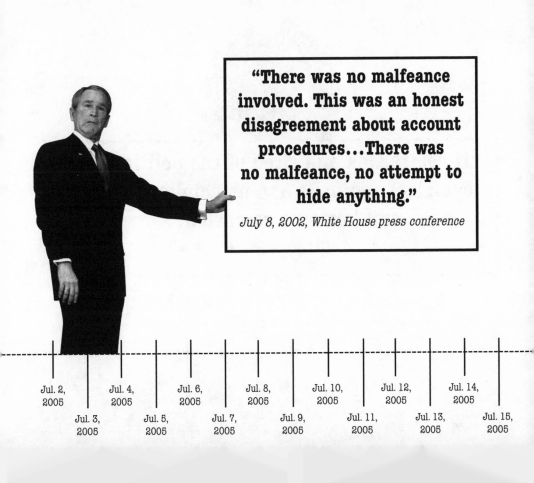

"There was no malfeance involved. This was an honest disagreement about account procedures...There was no malfeance, no attempt to hide anything."

July 8, 2002, White House press conference

Jul. 2, 2005

Jul. 3, 2005

Jul. 4, 2005

Jul. 5, 2005

Jul. 6, 2005

Jul. 7, 2005

Jul. 8, 2005

Jul. 9, 2005

Jul. 10, 2005

Jul. 11, 2005

Jul. 12, 2005

Jul. 13, 2005

Jul. 14, 2005

Jul. 15, 2005

> ## "If you're sick and tired of the politics of cynicism and polls and principles, come and join this campaign."
>
> *February 16, 2000, Hilton Head, South Carolina*

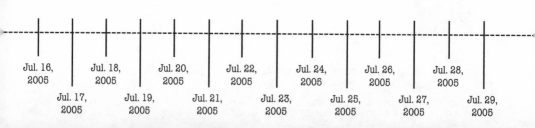

Jul. 16, 2005   Jul. 18, 2005   Jul. 20, 2005   Jul. 22, 2005   Jul. 24, 2005   Jul. 26, 2005   Jul. 28, 2005

Jul. 17, 2005   Jul. 19, 2005   Jul. 21, 2005   Jul. 23, 2005   Jul. 25, 2005   Jul. 27, 2005   Jul. 29, 2005

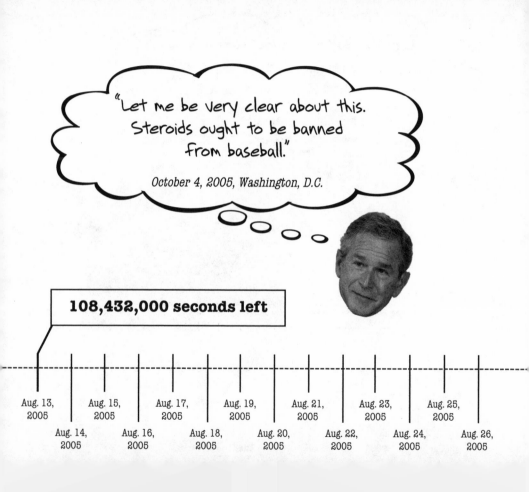

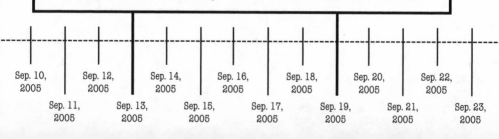

"I glance at the headlines just to kind of get a flavor for what's moving. I rarely read the stories, and get briefed by people who are probably read the news themselves."

September 21, 2003, Washington, D.C.

"If it were to rain a lot, there is concern from the Army Corps of Engineers that the levees might break. And so, therefore, we're cautious about encouraging people to return at this moment of history."

Washington, D.C.

"And to the extent that the federal government didn't fully do its job right, I take responsibility."

White House speech, referring to the Hurricane Katrina relief disaster

Sep. 10, 2005 | Sep. 11, 2005 | Sep. 12, 2005 | Sep. 13, 2005 | Sep. 14, 2005 | Sep. 15, 2005 | Sep. 16, 2005 | Sep. 17, 2005 | Sep. 18, 2005 | Sep. 19, 2005 | Sep. 20, 2005 | Sep. 21, 2005 | Sep. 22, 2005 | Sep. 23, 2005

"See, free nations are peaceful nations. Free nations don't attack each other. Free nations don't develop weapons of mass destruction."

October 3, 2003, Milwaukee, Wisconsin

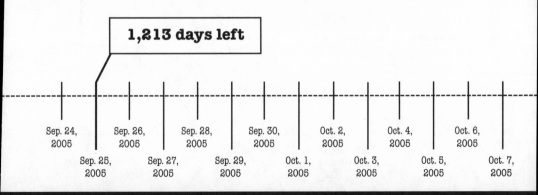

1,213 days left

Sep. 24, 2005 | Sep. 26, 2005 | Sep. 28, 2005 | Sep. 30, 2005 | Oct. 2, 2005 | Oct. 4, 2005 | Oct. 6, 2005

Sep. 25, 2005 | Sep. 27, 2005 | Sep. 29, 2005 | Oct. 1, 2005 | Oct. 3, 2005 | Oct. 5, 2005 | Oct. 7, 2005

"We discussed the way forward in Iraq, discussed the importance of a democracy in the greater Middle East in order to leave behind a peaceful tomorrow."

May 10, 2005, Tbilisi, Georgia

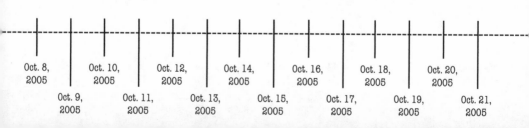

Oct. 8, 2005

Oct. 9, 2005

Oct. 10, 2005

Oct. 11, 2005

Oct. 12, 2005

Oct. 13, 2005

Oct. 14, 2005

Oct. 15, 2005

Oct. 16, 2005

Oct. 17, 2005

Oct. 18, 2005

Oct. 19, 2005

Oct. 20, 2005

Oct. 21, 2005

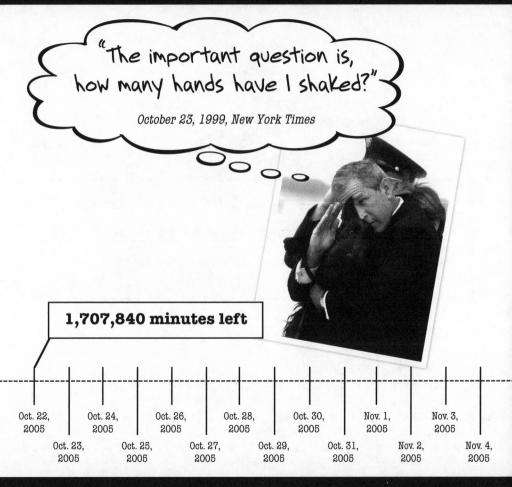

"The important question is, how many hands have I shaked?"

October 23, 1999, New York Times

1,707,840 minutes left

Oct. 22, 2005
Oct. 23, 2005
Oct. 24, 2005
Oct. 25, 2005
Oct. 26, 2005
Oct. 27, 2005
Oct. 28, 2005
Oct. 29, 2005
Oct. 30, 2005
Oct. 31, 2005
Nov. 1, 2005
Nov. 2, 2005
Nov. 3, 2005
Nov. 4, 2005

> ## "As a matter of fact, I know relations between our governments is good."
>
> *Washington, D.C., speaking about relations between the U.S. and South Korea*

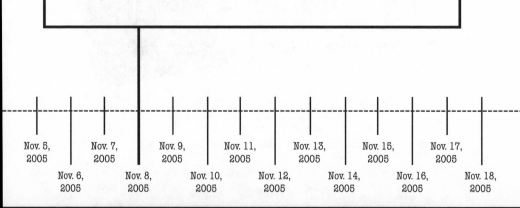

Nov. 5, 2005	Nov. 7, 2005	Nov. 9, 2005

Nov. 5, 2005   Nov. 7, 2005   Nov. 9, 2005   Nov. 11, 2005   Nov. 13, 2005   Nov. 15, 2005   Nov. 17, 2005

Nov. 6, 2005   Nov. 8, 2005   Nov. 10, 2005   Nov. 12, 2005   Nov. 14, 2005   Nov. 16, 2005   Nov. 18, 2005

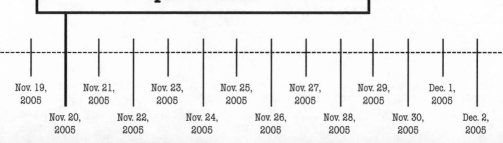

George Bush tries to leave a Beijing press conference and cannot open the door.

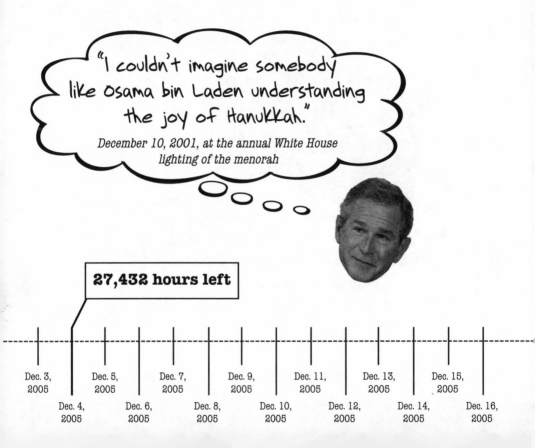

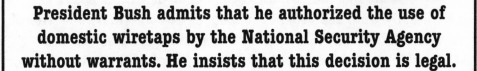

"Natural gas is hemispheric.
I like to call it hemispheric in nature because
it is a product that we can find
in our neighborhoods."

December 20, 2000, Washington, D.C.

President Bush admits that he authorized the use of domestic wiretaps by the National Security Agency without warrants. He insists that this decision is legal.

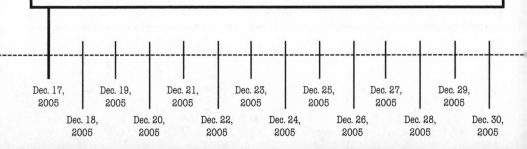

Dec. 17, 2005

Dec. 18, 2005

Dec. 19, 2005

Dec. 20, 2005

Dec. 21, 2005

Dec. 22, 2005

Dec. 23, 2005

Dec. 24, 2005

Dec. 25, 2005

Dec. 26, 2005

Dec. 27, 2005

Dec. 28, 2005

Dec. 29, 2005

Dec. 30, 2005

"I was a prisoner, too, but for bad reasons."

January 13, 2004, Monterrey, Mexico, to President Nestor Kirchner of Argentina upon learning that he was once a prisoner of the old regime

"As you can possibly see, I have an injury myself—not here at the hospital, but in combat with a cedar. I eventually won. The cedar gave me a little scratch. As a matter of fact, the Colonel asked if I needed first aid when she first saw me. I was able to avoid any major surgical operations here, but thanks for your compassion, Colonel."

At the Amputee Care Center of Brooke Army Medical Center

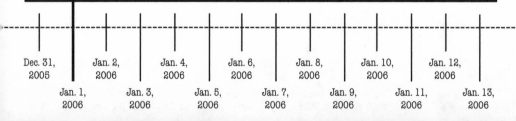

| Dec. 31, 2005 | Jan. 1, 2006 | Jan. 2, 2006 | Jan. 3, 2006 | Jan. 4, 2006 | Jan. 5, 2006 | Jan. 6, 2006 | Jan. 7, 2006 | Jan. 8, 2006 | Jan. 9, 2006 | Jan. 10, 2006 | Jan. 11, 2006 | Jan. 12, 2006 | Jan. 13, 2006 |

"Because he's hiding."

*January 14, 2005, aboard Air Force One, speaking about
why Osama bin Laden is still at large*

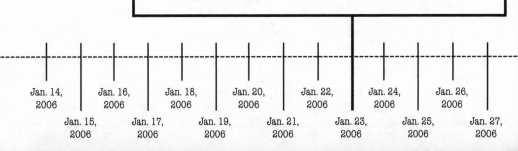

**"I'll be glad to talk about ranching, but I haven't
seen the movie. I've heard about it. I hope you
go—you know—I hope you go back to the ranch
and the farm is what I'm about to say."**

Manhattan, Kansas, discussing the film Brokeback Mountain

Jan. 14,
2006

Jan. 15,
2006

Jan. 16,
2006

Jan. 17,
2006

Jan. 18,
2006

Jan. 19,
2006

Jan. 20,
2006

Jan. 21,
2006

Jan. 22,
2006

Jan. 23,
2006

Jan. 24,
2006

Jan. 25,
2006

Jan. 26,
2006

Jan. 27,
2006

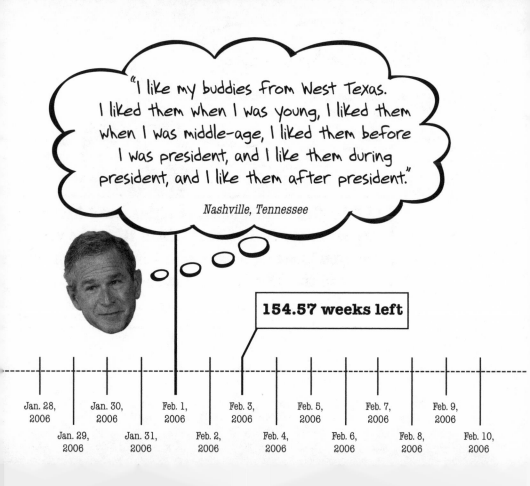

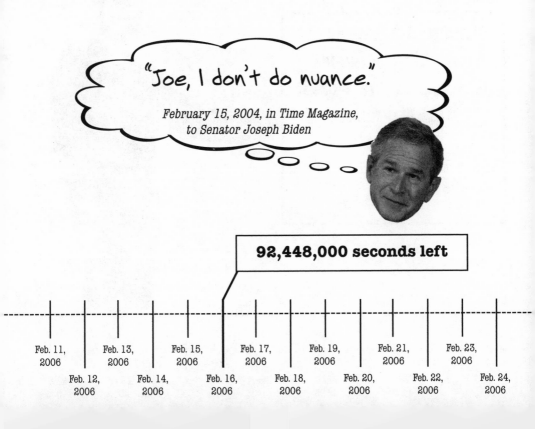

> "Ann and I will carry out this equivocal message to the world: Markets must be open."

March 2, 2001, swearing in Ann Veneman as the Secretary of Agriculture

Feb. 25,
2006

Feb. 26,
2006

Feb. 27,
2006

Feb. 28,
2006

Mar. 1,
2006

Mar. 2,
2006

Mar. 3,
2006

Mar. 4,
2006

Mar. 5,
2006

Mar. 6,
2006

Mar. 7,
2006

Mar. 8,
2006

Mar. 9,
2006

Mar. 10,
2006

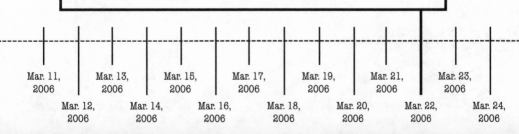

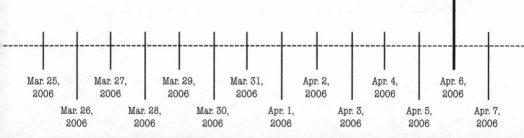

"I strongly believe we're doing the right thing. If I didn't believe it—I'm going to repeat what I said before—I'd pull the troops out, nor if I believed we could win, I would pull the troops out."

Charlotte, North Carolina

Mar. 25, 2006

Mar. 26, 2006

Mar. 27, 2006

Mar. 28, 2006

Mar. 29, 2006

Mar. 30, 2006

Mar. 31, 2006

Apr. 1, 2006

Apr. 2, 2006

Apr. 3, 2006

Apr. 4, 2006

Apr. 5, 2006

Apr. 6, 2006

Apr. 7, 2006

"I aim to be a competitive nation."

San Jose, California

"I'm going to spend a lot of time on Social Security. I enjoy it. I enjoy taking on the issue. I guess it's the mother in me."

April 14, 2005, Washington, D.C.

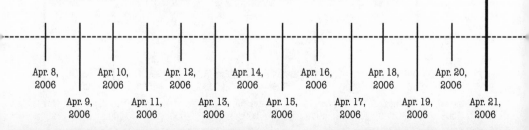

Apr. 8, 2006
Apr. 9, 2006
Apr. 10, 2006
Apr. 11, 2006
Apr. 12, 2006
Apr. 13, 2006
Apr. 14, 2006
Apr. 15, 2006
Apr. 16, 2006
Apr. 17, 2006
Apr. 18, 2006
Apr. 19, 2006
Apr. 20, 2006
Apr. 21, 2006

"I can look you in the eye and tell you I feel I've tried to solve the problem diplomatically to the max, and would have committed troops both in Afghanistan and Iraq, knowing what I know today."

Irvine, California

"The point now is how do we work together to achieve important goals. And one such goal is a democracy in Germany."

Washington, D.C.

Apr. 22, 2006 — Apr. 23, 2006 — Apr. 24, 2006 — Apr. 25, 2006 — Apr. 26, 2006 — Apr. 27, 2006 — Apr. 28, 2006 — Apr. 29, 2006 — Apr. 30, 2006 — May 1, 2006 — May 2, 2006 — May 3, 2006 — May 4, 2006 — May 5, 2006

"Like you, I have been disgraced about what I've seen on TV that took place in [Abu Ghraib] prison."

May 13, 2004, Parkersburg, West Virginia

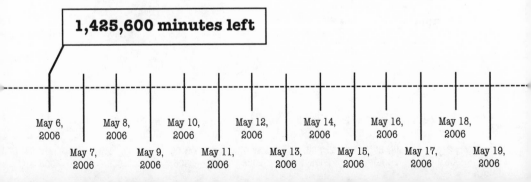

1,425,600 minutes left

May 6,
2006

May 7,
2006

May 8,
2006

May 9,
2006

May 10,
2006

May 11,
2006

May 12,
2006

May 13,
2006

May 14,
2006

May 15,
2006

May 16,
2006

May 17,
2006

May 18,
2006

May 19,
2006

"Trying to stop suiciders—
which we're doing a pretty good job of
on occasion—is difficult to do. And what the
Iraqis are going to have to eventually do
is convince those who are conducting suiciders
who are not inspired by Al Qaeda, for example, to
realize there's a peaceful tomorrow."

Washington, D.C.

23,424 hours left

May 20,
2006

May 21,
2006

May 22,
2006

May 23,
2006

May 24,
2006

May 25,
2006

May 26,
2006

May 27,
2006

May 28,
2006

May 29,
2006

May 30,
2006

May 31,
2006

Jun. 1,
2006

Jun. 2,
2006

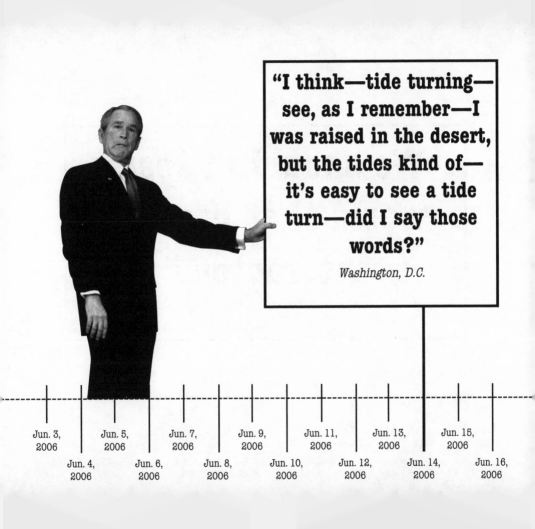

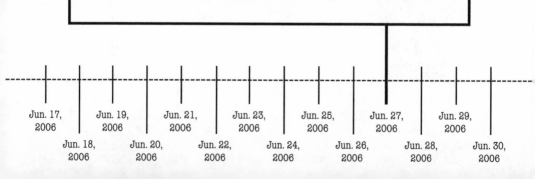

"We shouldn't fear a world that is more interacted."

Washington, D.C.

Jun. 17, 2006 Jun. 19, 2006 Jun. 21, 2006 Jun. 23, 2006 Jun. 25, 2006 Jun. 27, 2006 Jun. 29, 2006

Jun. 18, 2006 Jun. 20, 2006 Jun. 22, 2006 Jun. 24, 2006 Jun. 26, 2006 Jun. 28, 2006 Jun. 30, 2006

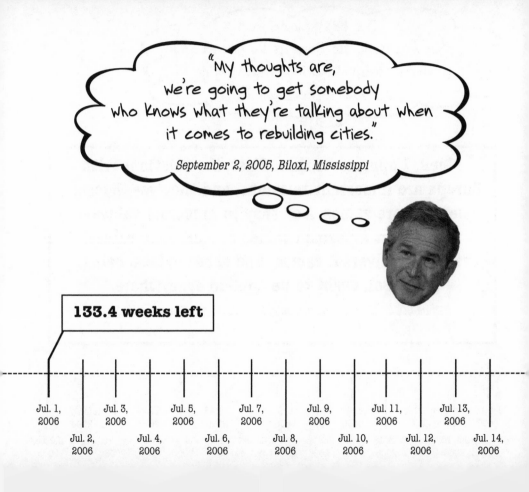

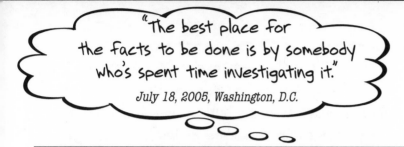

"The best place for the facts to be done is by somebody who's spent time investigating it."

July 18, 2005, Washington, D.C.

"Well, I appreciate that. First, the relations with Europe are important relations, and they've—because we do share values. And they're universal values— they're not American values or European values, they're universal values. And those values, being universal, ought to be applied everywhere."

June 20, 2005, European Union press conference, Washington, D.C.

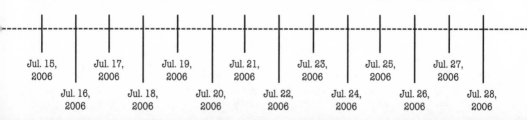

Jul. 15, 2006   Jul. 17, 2006   Jul. 19, 2006   Jul. 21, 2006   Jul. 23, 2006   Jul. 25, 2006   Jul. 27, 2006

Jul. 16, 2006   Jul. 18, 2006   Jul. 20, 2006   Jul. 22, 2006   Jul. 24, 2006   Jul. 26, 2006   Jul. 28, 2006

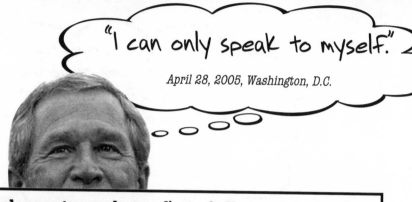

"I can only speak to myself."

April 28, 2005, Washington, D.C.

"I think younger workers—first of all, younger workers
have been promised benefits the government—promises
that have been promised, benefits that we can't keep.
That's just the way it is."

May 4, 2005, Washington, D.C.

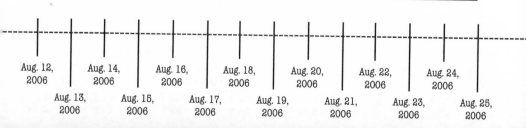

Aug. 12,
2006

Aug. 13,
2006

Aug. 14,
2006

Aug. 15,
2006

Aug. 16,
2006

Aug. 17,
2006

Aug. 18,
2006

Aug. 19,
2006

Aug. 20,
2006

Aug. 21,
2006

Aug. 22,
2006

Aug. 23,
2006

Aug. 24,
2006

Aug. 25,
2006

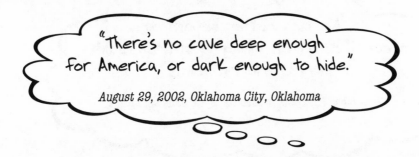

"There's no cave deep enough for America, or dark enough to hide."

August 29, 2002, Oklahoma City, Oklahoma

"I can't wait to join you in the joy of welcoming neighbors back into neighborhoods, and small businesses up and running, and cutting those ribbons that somebody is creating new jobs."

September 5, 2005, Poplarville, Mississippi

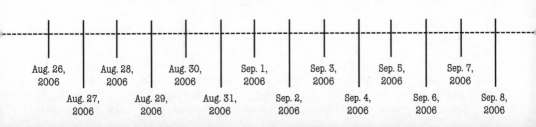

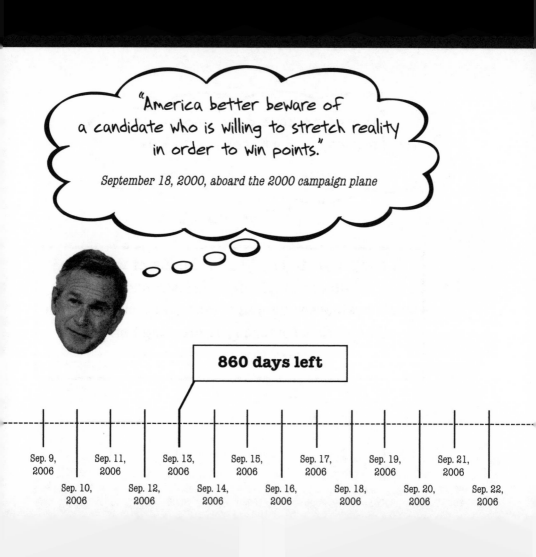

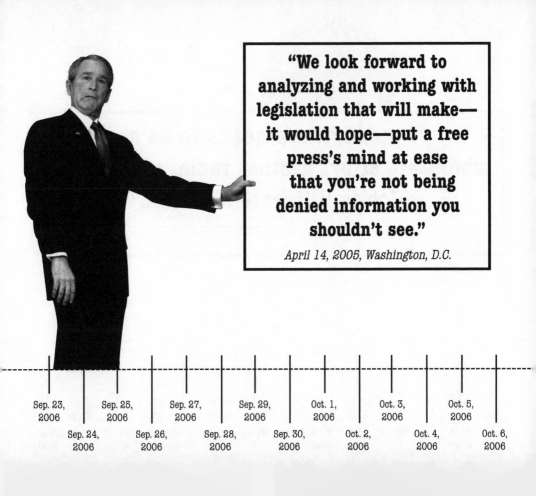

> ## "I mean, there needs to be a wholesale effort against racial profiling, which is illiterate children."
>
> *October 11, 2000, second presidential debate*

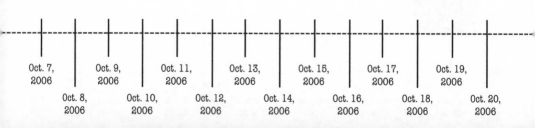

Oct. 7, 2006

Oct. 8, 2006

Oct. 9, 2006

Oct. 10, 2006

Oct. 11, 2006

Oct. 12, 2006

Oct. 13, 2006

Oct. 14, 2006

Oct. 15, 2006

Oct. 16, 2006

Oct. 17, 2006

Oct. 18, 2006

Oct. 19, 2006

Oct. 20, 2006

> "I don't want nations feeling like that they can bully ourselves and our allies. I want to have a ballistic defense system so that we can make the world more peaceful, and at the same time I want to reduce our own nuclear capacities to the level commiserate with keeping the peace."
>
> *October 23, 2000, Des Moines, Iowa*

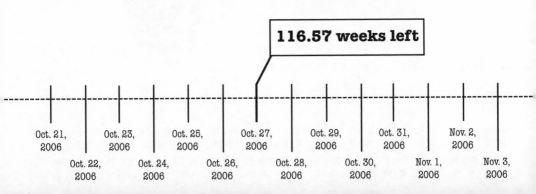

116.57 weeks left

Oct. 21, 2006   Oct. 22, 2006   Oct. 23, 2006   Oct. 24, 2006   Oct. 25, 2006   Oct. 26, 2006   Oct. 27, 2006   Oct. 28, 2006   Oct. 29, 2006   Oct. 30, 2006   Oct. 31, 2006   Nov. 1, 2006   Nov. 2, 2006   Nov. 3, 2006

"The folks who conducted to act on our country on September 11th made a big mistake. They underestimated America. They underestimated our resolve, our determination, our love for freedom. They misunderestimated the fact that we love a neighbor in need. They misunderestimated the compassion of our country. I think they misunderestimated the will and determination of the Commander-in-Chief, too."

September 26, 2001, Washington, D.C.

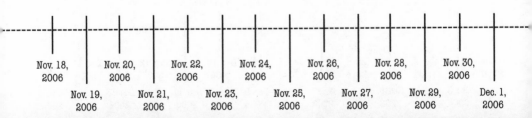

Nov. 18, 2006

Nov. 19, 2006

Nov. 20, 2006

Nov. 21, 2006

Nov. 22, 2006

Nov. 23, 2006

Nov. 24, 2006

Nov. 25, 2006

Nov. 26, 2006

Nov. 27, 2006

Nov. 28, 2006

Nov. 29, 2006

Nov. 30, 2006

Dec. 1, 2006

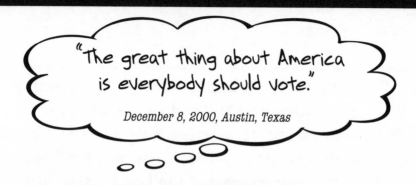

"The great thing about America is everybody should vote."

December 8, 2000, Austin, Texas

"It's good to see so many friends here in the Rose Garden. This is our first event in this beautiful spot, and it's appropriate we talk about policy that will affect people's lives in a positive way in such a beautiful, beautiful part of our national—really, our national park system, my guess is you would want to call it."

February 28, 2001, speech in the Rose Garden

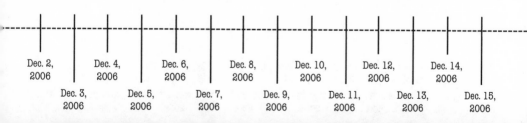

Dec. 2, 2006
Dec. 3, 2006
Dec. 4, 2006
Dec. 5, 2006
Dec. 6, 2006
Dec. 7, 2006
Dec. 8, 2006
Dec. 9, 2006
Dec. 10, 2006
Dec. 11, 2006
Dec. 12, 2006
Dec. 13, 2006
Dec. 14, 2006
Dec. 15, 2006

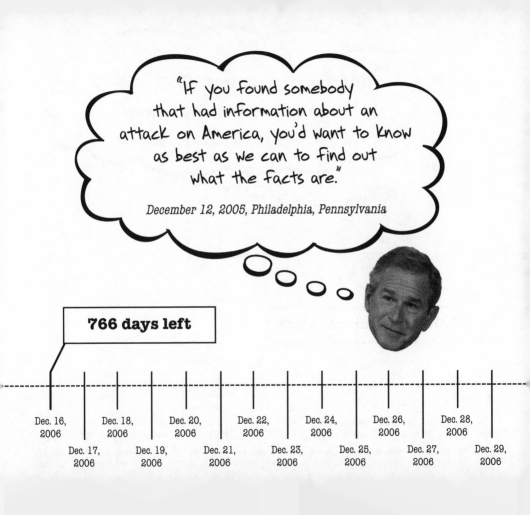

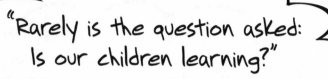

"Rarely is the question asked: Is our children learning?"

January 11, 2000, South Carolina campaign stop

1,072,800 minutes left

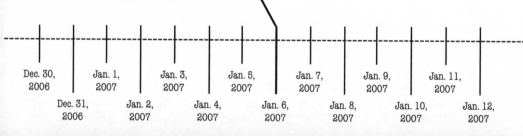

Dec. 30, 2006 • Dec. 31, 2006 • Jan. 1, 2007 • Jan. 2, 2007 • Jan. 3, 2007 • Jan. 4, 2007 • Jan. 5, 2007 • Jan. 6, 2007 • Jan. 7, 2007 • Jan. 8, 2007 • Jan. 9, 2007 • Jan. 10, 2007 • Jan. 11, 2007 • Jan. 12, 2007

"I want everybody to hear loud and clear that I'm going to be the president of everybody."

January 18, 2001, Washington, D.C.

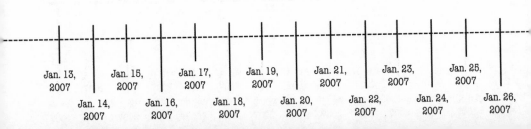

Jan. 13, 2007

Jan. 14, 2007

Jan. 15, 2007

Jan. 16, 2007

Jan. 17, 2007

Jan. 18, 2007

Jan. 19, 2007

Jan. 20, 2007

Jan. 21, 2007

Jan. 22, 2007

Jan. 23, 2007

Jan. 24, 2007

Jan. 25, 2007

Jan. 26, 2007

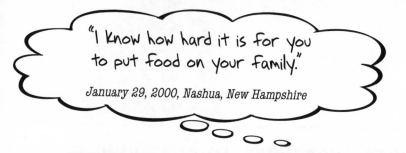

"I know how hard it is for you to put food on your family."

January 29, 2000, Nashua, New Hampshire

"One reason I like to highlight reading is, reading is the beginnings of the ability to be a good student. And if you can't read, it's going to be hard to realize dreams; it's going to be hard to go to college. So when your teachers say, read—you ought to listen to her."

February 9, 2001, Nalle Elementary School, Washington, D.C.

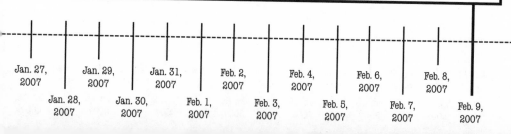

Jan. 27, 2007

Jan. 28, 2007

Jan. 29, 2007

Jan. 30, 2007

Jan. 31, 2007

Feb. 1, 2007

Feb. 2, 2007

Feb. 3, 2007

Feb. 4, 2007

Feb. 5, 2007

Feb. 6, 2007

Feb. 7, 2007

Feb. 8, 2007

Feb. 9, 2007

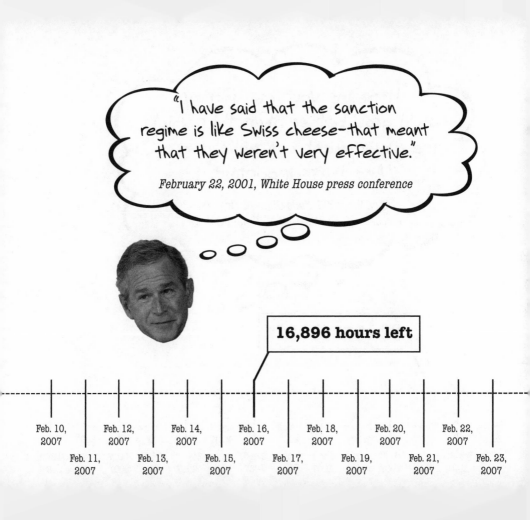

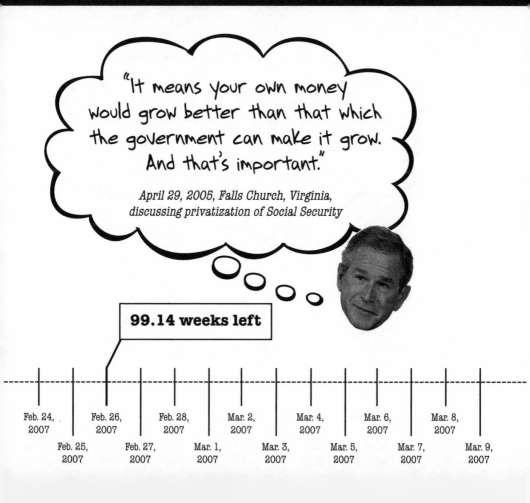

> "I like the idea of people running for office.
> There's a positive effect when you run for office.
> Maybe some will run for office and say, vote for me,
> I look forward to blowing up America. I don't know,
> I don't know if that will be their platform or not.
> But it's—I don't think so.
> I think people who generally run for office say,
> vote for me, I'm looking forward to fixing your potholes,
> or making sure you got bread on the table."

March 16, 2005, Washington, D.C., about the Middle East elections

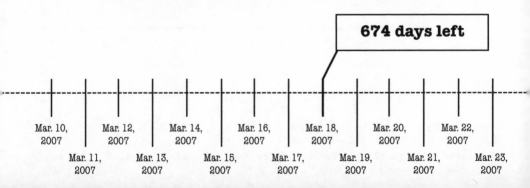

674 days left

Mar. 10, 2007 Mar. 12, 2007 Mar. 14, 2007 Mar. 16, 2007 Mar. 18, 2007 Mar. 20, 2007 Mar. 22, 2007

Mar. 11, 2007 Mar. 13, 2007 Mar. 15, 2007 Mar. 17, 2007 Mar. 19, 2007 Mar. 21, 2007 Mar. 23, 2007

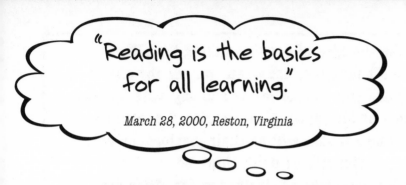

"Reading is the basics for all learning."

March 28, 2000, Reston, Virginia

Former Secretary of State Colin Powell's birthday.
"I try to be the same person I was yesterday."
—Colin Powell

Born on April 5, 1937

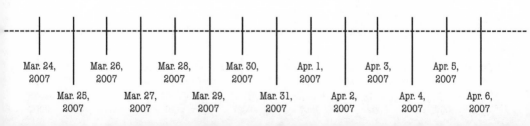

| Mar. 24, 2007 | Mar. 26, 2007 | Mar. 28, 2007 | Mar. 30, 2007 | Apr. 1, 2007 | Apr. 3, 2007 | Apr. 5, 2007 |
| Mar. 25, 2007 | Mar. 27, 2007 | Mar. 29, 2007 | Mar. 31, 2007 | Apr. 2, 2007 | Apr. 4, 2007 | Apr. 6, 2007 |

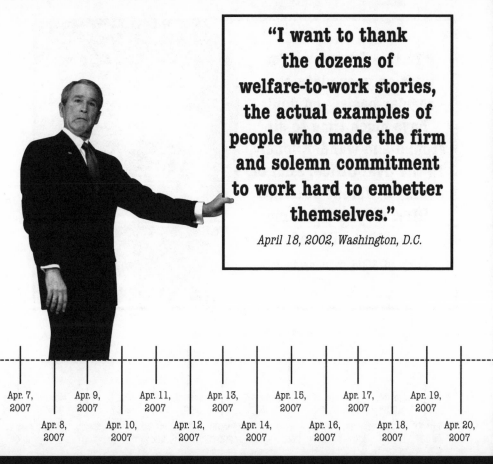

"I want to thank
the dozens of
welfare-to-work stories,
the actual examples of
people who made the firm
and solemn commitment
to work hard to embetter
themselves."

April 18, 2002, Washington, D.C.

| Apr. 7, 2007 | Apr. 9, 2007 | Apr. 11, 2007 | Apr. 13, 2007 | Apr. 15, 2007 | Apr. 17, 2007 | Apr. 19, 2007 |
| Apr. 8, 2007 | Apr. 10, 2007 | Apr. 12, 2007 | Apr. 14, 2007 | Apr. 16, 2007 | Apr. 18, 2007 | Apr. 20, 2007 |

"In this job you've got a lot on your plate on a regular basis; you don't have much time to sit around and wander, lonely, in the Oval Office, kind of asking different portraits, 'How do you think my standing will be?'"

March 16, 2005, Washington, D.C.

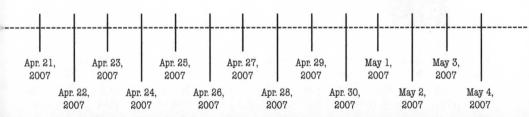

Apr. 21, 2007

Apr. 22, 2007

Apr. 23, 2007

Apr. 24, 2007

Apr. 25, 2007

Apr. 26, 2007

Apr. 27, 2007

Apr. 28, 2007

Apr. 29, 2007

Apr. 30, 2007

May 1, 2007

May 2, 2007

May 3, 2007

May 4, 2007

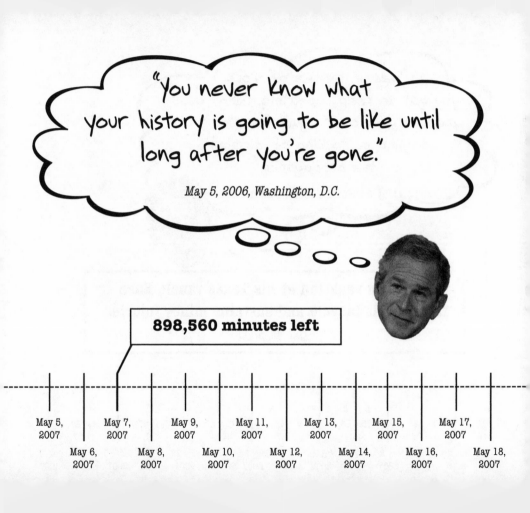

"See, in my line of work you got to keep repeating things over and over and over again for the truth to sink in, to kind of catapult the propaganda."

May 24, 2005, Greece, New York

While on vacation at his Texas ranch, Bush falls off his bicycle and sustains minor injuries.

May 22, 2004

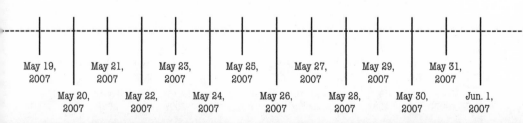

May 19, 2007   May 21, 2007   May 23, 2007   May 25, 2007   May 27, 2007   May 29, 2007   May 31, 2007

May 20, 2007   May 22, 2007   May 24, 2007   May 26, 2007   May 28, 2007   May 30, 2007   Jun. 1, 2007

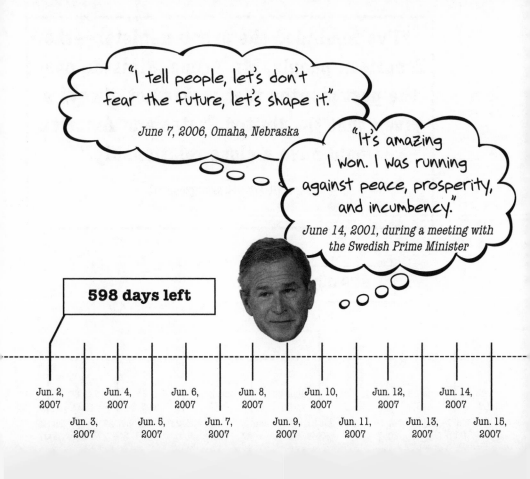

> ## "I've reminded the prime minister—the American people, Mr. Prime Minister, over the past months that it was not always a given that the United States and America would have a close relationship."
>
> *June 29, 2006, Washington, D.C.*

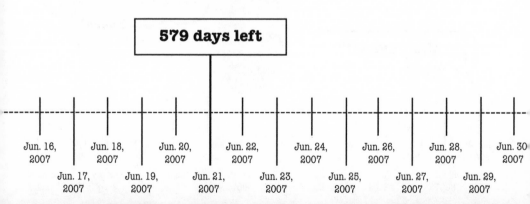

579 days left

Jun. 16, 2007	Jun. 18, 2007	Jun. 20, 2007	Jun. 22, 2007	Jun. 24, 2007	Jun. 26, 2007	Jun. 28, 2007	Jun. 30, 2007
Jun. 17, 2007	Jun. 19, 2007	Jun. 21, 2007	Jun. 23, 2007	Jun. 25, 2007	Jun. 27, 2007	Jun. 29, 2007	

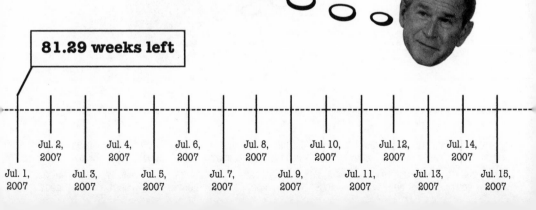

"No more public scatology."

July 18, 1997, in a personal note to future Supreme Court nominee Harriet Miers

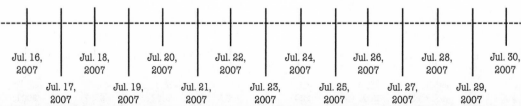

| Jul. 16, 2007 | Jul. 17, 2007 | Jul. 18, 2007 | Jul. 19, 2007 | Jul. 20, 2007 | Jul. 21, 2007 | Jul. 22, 2007 | Jul. 23, 2007 | Jul. 24, 2007 | Jul. 25, 2007 | Jul. 26, 2007 | Jul. 27, 2007 | Jul. 28, 2007 | Jul. 29, 2007 | Jul. 30, 2007 |

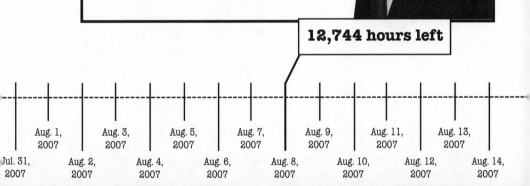

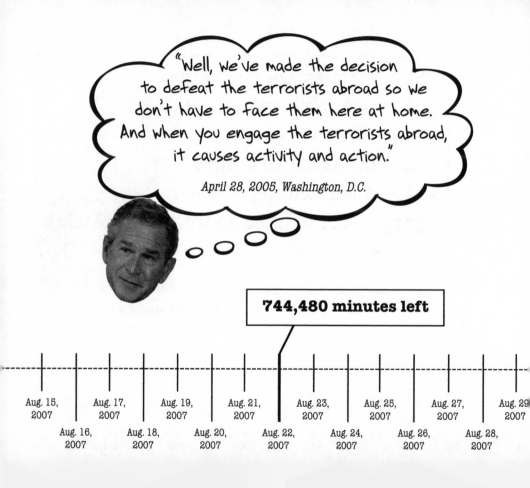

> "We'll let our friends be the peacekeepers and the great country called America will be the pacemakers."
>
> *September 6, 2000 in Houston, Texas*

> **"I am here to make an announcement that this Thursday, ticket counters and airplanes will fly out of Ronald Reagan Airport."**
>
> *October 3, 2001, Washington, D.C.*

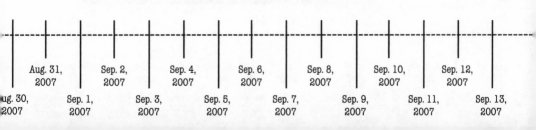

Aug. 30, 2007 · Aug. 31, 2007 · Sep. 1, 2007 · Sep. 2, 2007 · Sep. 3, 2007 · Sep. 4, 2007 · Sep. 5, 2007 · Sep. 6, 2007 · Sep. 7, 2007 · Sep. 8, 2007 · Sep. 9, 2007 · Sep. 10, 2007 · Sep. 11, 2007 · Sep. 12, 2007 · Sep. 13, 2007

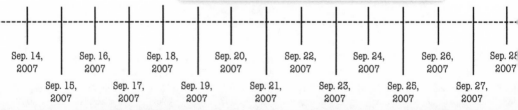

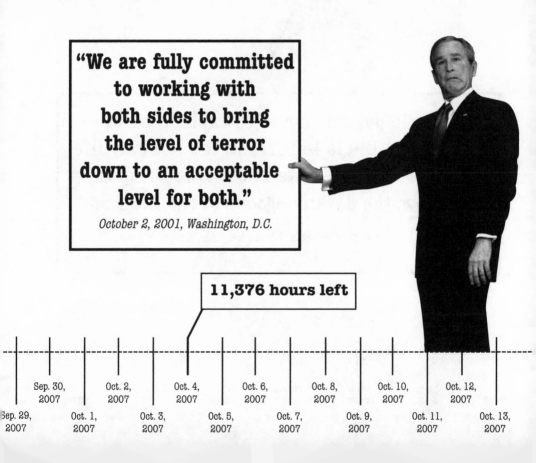

"It's important for us to explain to our nation that life is important. It's not only life of babies, but it's life of children living in, you know, the dark dungeons of the Internet."

October 24, 2000, Arlington Heights, Illinois

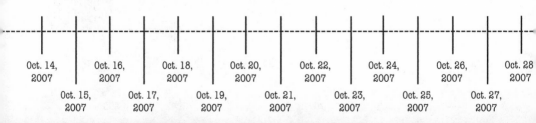

Oct. 14, 2007

Oct. 16, 2007

Oct. 18, 2007

Oct. 20, 2007

Oct. 22, 2007

Oct. 24, 2007

Oct. 26, 2007

Oct. 28, 2007

Oct. 15, 2007

Oct. 17, 2007

Oct. 19, 2007

Oct. 21, 2007

Oct. 23, 2007

Oct. 25, 2007

Oct. 27, 2007

"There's an old saying in Tennessee—I know it's in Texas, probably in Tennessee—that says, fool me once, shame on—shame on you. Fool me—you can't get fooled again."

September 17, 2002, Nashville, Tennessee

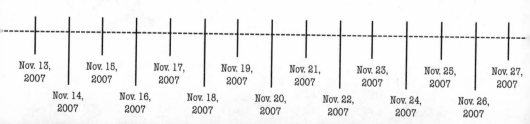

Nov. 13, 2007

Nov. 14, 2007

Nov. 15, 2007

Nov. 16, 2007

Nov. 17, 2007

Nov. 18, 2007

Nov. 19, 2007

Nov. 20, 2007

Nov. 21, 2007

Nov. 22, 2007

Nov. 23, 2007

Nov. 24, 2007

Nov. 25, 2007

Nov. 26, 2007

Nov. 27, 2007

"Sometimes, Washington is one of these towns where the person-people who think they've got the sharp elbow is the most effective person."

December 3, 2002, New Orleans, Louisiana

"Whether they be Christian, Jew, or Muslim, or Hindu, people have heard the universal call to love a neighbor just like they'd like to be called themselves."

October 8, 2003, Washington, D.C.

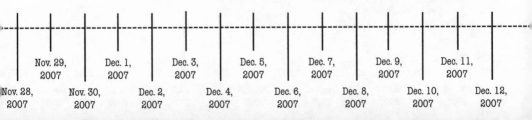

Nov. 28, 2007 · Nov. 29, 2007 · Nov. 30, 2007 · Dec. 1, 2007 · Dec. 2, 2007 · Dec. 3, 2007 · Dec. 4, 2007 · Dec. 5, 2007 · Dec. 6, 2007 · Dec. 7, 2007 · Dec. 8, 2007 · Dec. 9, 2007 · Dec. 10, 2007 · Dec. 11, 2007 · Dec. 12, 2007

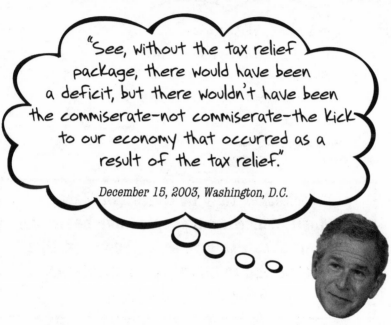

"See, without the tax relief package, there would have been a deficit, but there wouldn't have been the commiserate—not commiserate—the kick to our economy that occurred as a result of the tax relief."

December 15, 2003, Washington, D.C.

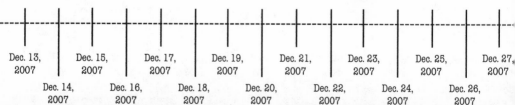

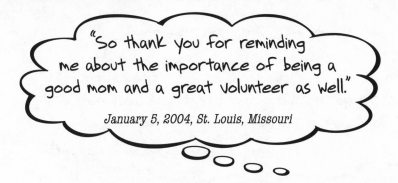

> "So thank you for reminding me about the importance of being a good mom and a great volunteer as well."

January 5, 2004, St. Louis, Missouri

> ## "I am mindful not only of preserving executive powers for myself, but for predecessors as well."

January 29, 2001, Washington, D.C.

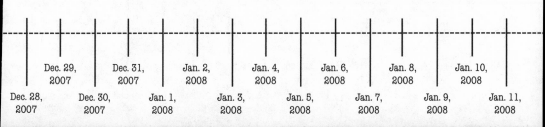

Dec. 28, 2007
Dec. 29, 2007
Dec. 30, 2007
Dec. 31, 2007
Jan. 1, 2008
Jan. 2, 2008
Jan. 3, 2008
Jan. 4, 2008
Jan. 5, 2008
Jan. 6, 2008
Jan. 7, 2008
Jan. 8, 2008
Jan. 9, 2008
Jan. 10, 2008
Jan. 11, 2008

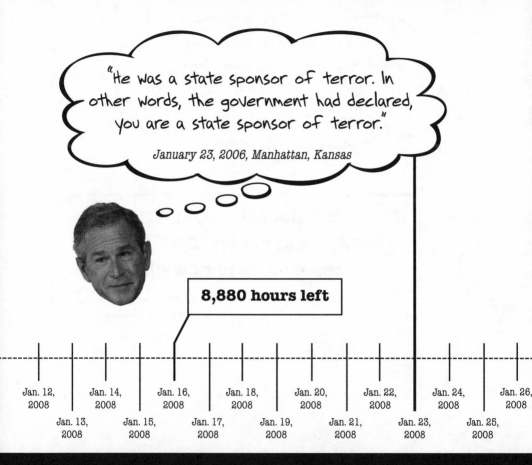

"He was a state sponsor of terror. In other words, the government had declared, you are a state sponsor of terror."

January 23, 2006, Manhattan, Kansas

8,880 hours left

Jan. 12, 2008
Jan. 13, 2008
Jan. 14, 2008
Jan. 15, 2008
Jan. 16, 2008
Jan. 17, 2008
Jan. 18, 2008
Jan. 19, 2008
Jan. 20, 2008
Jan. 21, 2008
Jan. 22, 2008
Jan. 23, 2008
Jan. 24, 2008
Jan. 25, 2008
Jan. 26, 2008

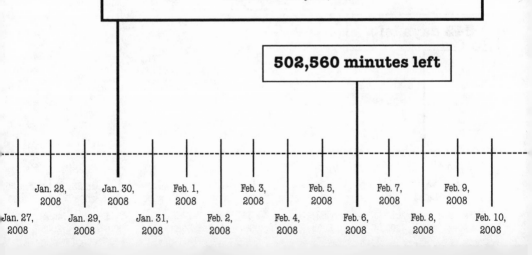

Vice President Dick Cheney's birthday.

"We will, in fact, be greeted as liberators."
—Dick Cheney

Born on January 30, 1941

502,560 minutes left

Jan. 27, 2008
Jan. 28, 2008
Jan. 29, 2008
Jan. 30, 2008
Jan. 31, 2008
Feb. 1, 2008
Feb. 2, 2008
Feb. 3, 2008
Feb. 4, 2008
Feb. 5, 2008
Feb. 6, 2008
Feb. 7, 2008
Feb. 8, 2008
Feb. 9, 2008
Feb. 10, 2008

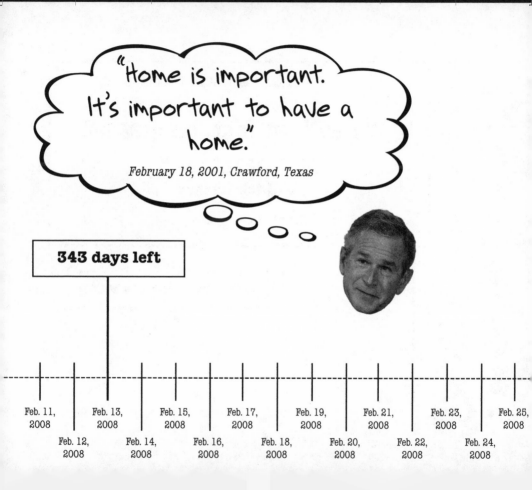

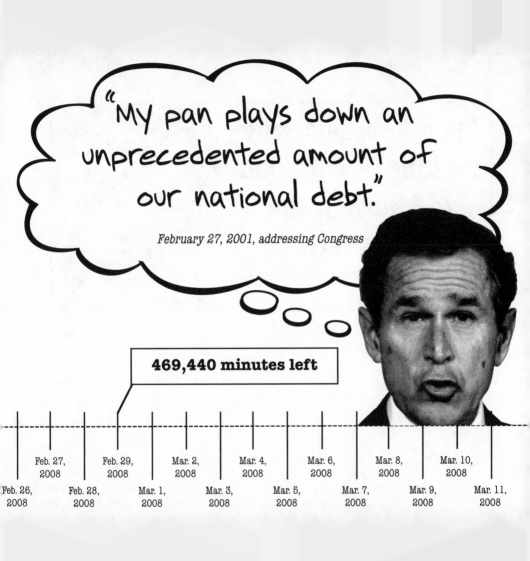

"[I'm] occasionally reading, I want you to know, in the second term."

March 16, 2005, Washington, D.C.

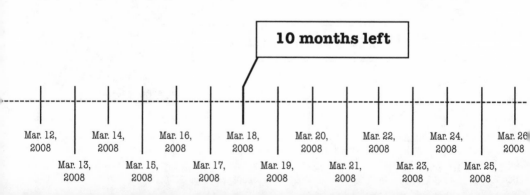

10 months left

Mar. 12, 2008

Mar. 13, 2008

Mar. 14, 2008

Mar. 15, 2008

Mar. 16, 2008

Mar. 17, 2008

Mar. 18, 2008

Mar. 19, 2008

Mar. 20, 2008

Mar. 21, 2008

Mar. 22, 2008

Mar. 23, 2008

Mar. 24, 2008

Mar. 25, 2008

Mar. 26, 2008

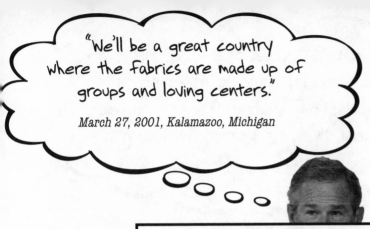

"We'll be a great country where the fabrics are made up of groups and loving centers."

March 27, 2001, Kalamazoo, Michigan

Former majority leader Tom DeLay's birthday.
"It has never been proven that air toxins are hazardous to people." —Tom DeLay

Born on April 8, 1947

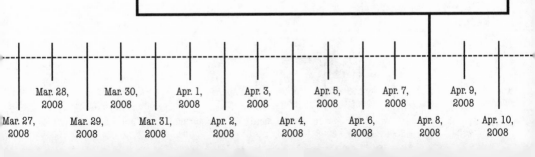

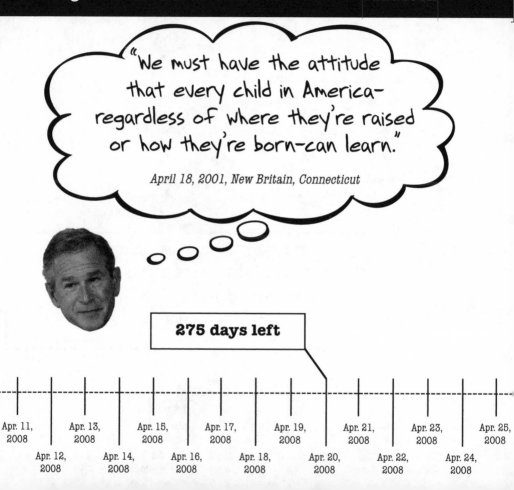

"We must have the attitude that every child in America—regardless of where they're raised or how they're born—can learn."

April 18, 2001, New Britain, Connecticut

275 days left

Apr. 11, 2008
Apr. 12, 2008
Apr. 13, 2008
Apr. 14, 2008
Apr. 15, 2008
Apr. 16, 2008
Apr. 17, 2008
Apr. 18, 2008
Apr. 19, 2008
Apr. 20, 2008
Apr. 21, 2008
Apr. 22, 2008
Apr. 23, 2008
Apr. 24, 2008
Apr. 25, 2008

> **"I hope we get to the bottom of the answer. It's what I'm interested to know."**
>
> *April 26, 2000, Associated Press*

> Former Attorney General John Ashcroft's birthday.
> **"24/7—24 hours a week, 7 months a year." —John Ashcroft**
>
> *Born on May 9, 1942*

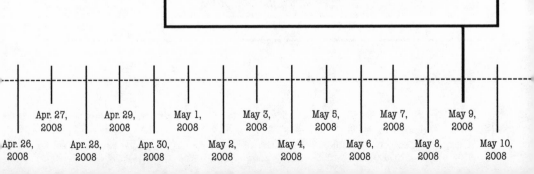

| Apr. 26, 2008 | Apr. 27, 2008 | Apr. 28, 2008 | Apr. 29, 2008 | Apr. 30, 2008 | May 1, 2008 | May 2, 2008 | May 3, 2008 | May 4, 2008 | May 5, 2008 | May 6, 2008 | May 7, 2008 | May 8, 2008 | May 9, 2008 | May 10, 2008 |

"**That's George Washington, the first president, of course. The interesting thing about him is that I read three—three or four books about him last year. Isn't that interesting?**"

May 5, 2006, the Oval Office

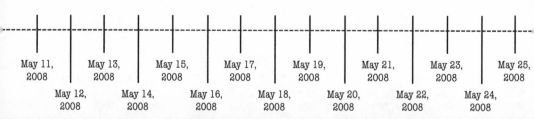

May 11, 2008

May 12, 2008

May 13, 2008

May 14, 2008

May 15, 2008

May 16, 2008

May 17, 2008

May 18, 2008

May 19, 2008

May 20, 2008

May 21, 2008

May 22, 2008

May 23, 2008

May 24, 2008

May 25, 2008

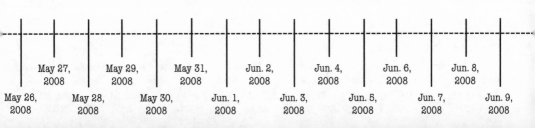

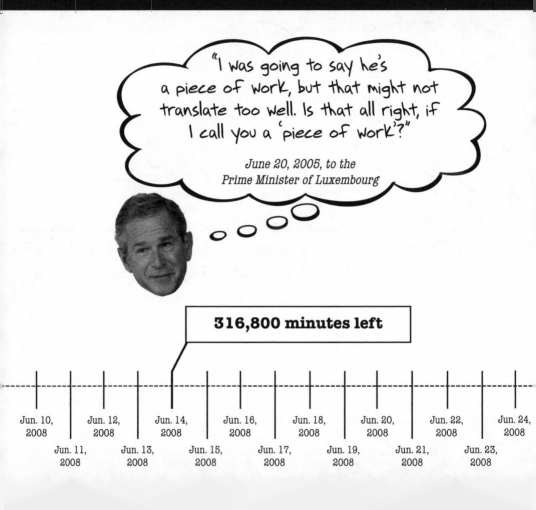

George W. Bush's birthday.

"We want to restore honor and integrity to the White House."

Born on July 6, 1946

208 days left

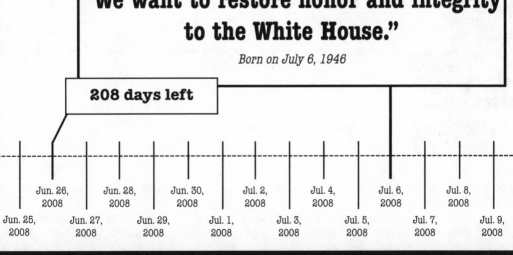

Jun. 25, 2008 · Jun. 26, 2008 · Jun. 27, 2008 · Jun. 28, 2008 · Jun. 29, 2008 · Jun. 30, 2008 · Jul. 1, 2008 · Jul. 2, 2008 · Jul. 3, 2008 · Jul. 4, 2008 · Jul. 5, 2008 · Jul. 6, 2008 · Jul. 7, 2008 · Jul. 8, 2008 · Jul. 9, 2008

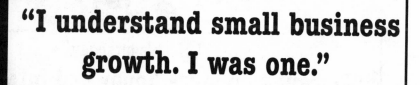

"I understand small business growth. I was one."

February 19, 2000, New York Daily News

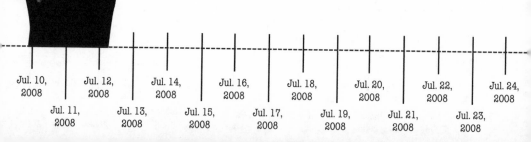

Jul. 10, 2008	Jul. 12, 2008	Jul. 14, 2008	Jul. 16, 2008	Jul. 18, 2008	Jul. 20, 2008	Jul. 22, 2008	Jul. 24, 2008
Jul. 11, 2008	Jul. 13, 2008	Jul. 15, 2008	Jul. 17, 2008	Jul. 19, 2008	Jul. 21, 2008	Jul. 23, 2008	

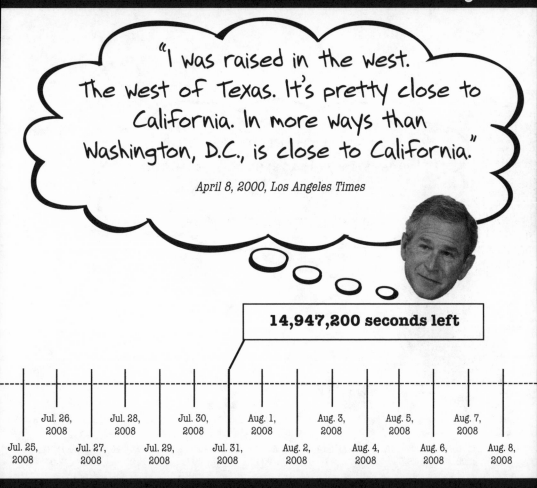

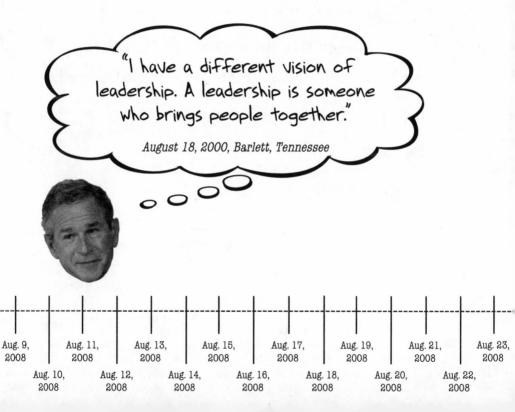

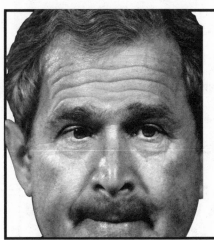

"Laura and I don't realize how bright our children is sometimes until we get an objective analysis."

April 15, 2000, CNBC

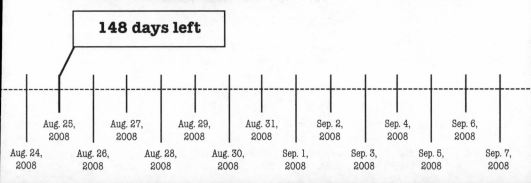

148 days left

| Aug. 24, 2008 | Aug. 25, 2008 | Aug. 26, 2008 | Aug. 27, 2008 | Aug. 28, 2008 | Aug. 29, 2008 | Aug. 30, 2008 | Aug. 31, 2008 | Sep. 1, 2008 | Sep. 2, 2008 | Sep. 3, 2008 | Sep. 4, 2008 | Sep. 5, 2008 | Sep. 6, 2008 | Sep. 7, 2008 |

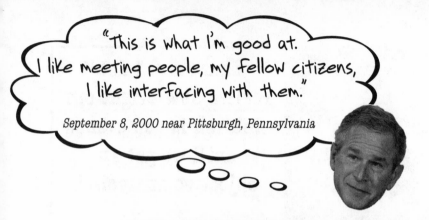

"This is what I'm good at.
I like meeting people, my fellow citizens,
I like interfacing with them."

September 8, 2000 near Pittsburgh, Pennsylvania

> ## "I am a person who recognizes the fallacy of humans."
>
> *September 19, 2000, the Oprah Winfrey Show*

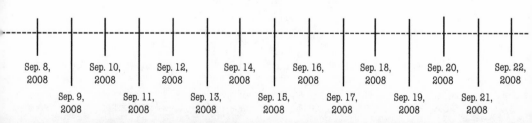

Sep. 8, 2008

Sep. 9, 2008

Sep. 10, 2008

Sep. 11, 2008

Sep. 12, 2008

Sep. 13, 2008

Sep. 14, 2008

Sep. 15, 2008

Sep. 16, 2008

Sep. 17, 2008

Sep. 18, 2008

Sep. 19, 2008

Sep. 20, 2008

Sep. 21, 2008

Sep. 22, 2008

"We need to counter the shockwave of the evildoer by having individual rate cuts accelerated and by thinking about tax rebates."

October 4, 2001, Washington, D.C.

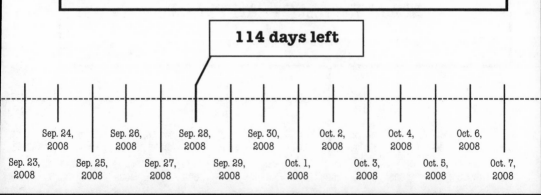

114 days left

| Sep. 23, 2008 | Sep. 24, 2008 | Sep. 25, 2008 | Sep. 26, 2008 | Sep. 27, 2008 | Sep. 28, 2008 | Sep. 29, 2008 | Sep. 30, 2008 | Oct. 1, 2008 | Oct. 2, 2008 | Oct. 3, 2008 | Oct. 4, 2008 | Oct. 5, 2008 | Oct. 6, 2008 | Oct. 7, 2008 |

"I hear there's rumors on the Internets that we're going to have a draft."

October 8, 2004, St. Louis, Missouri
(second presidential debate)

Former White House Press Secretary Ari Fleischer's birthday.

"There is already a mountain of evidence that Saddam Hussein is gathering weapons...adding additional information is like adding a foot to Mount Everest." —Ari Fleischer

Born on October 13, 1960

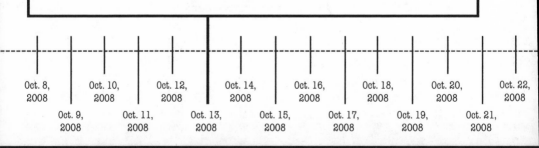

| Oct. 8, 2008 | Oct. 10, 2008 | Oct. 12, 2008 | Oct. 14, 2008 | Oct. 16, 2008 | Oct. 18, 2008 | Oct. 20, 2008 | Oct. 22, 2008 |

| Oct. 9, 2008 | Oct. 11, 2008 | Oct. 13, 2008 | Oct. 15, 2008 | Oct. 17, 2008 | Oct. 19, 2008 | Oct. 21, 2008 |

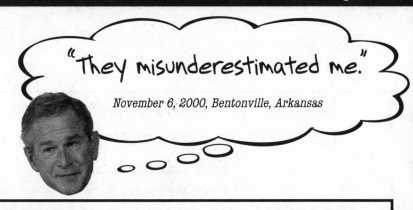

"They misunderestimated me."

November 6, 2000, Bentonville, Arkansas

After Bush is reelected, *The Daily Mirror* asks on its cover: "How can 59,054,087 Americans be so dumb?"

November 4, 2004

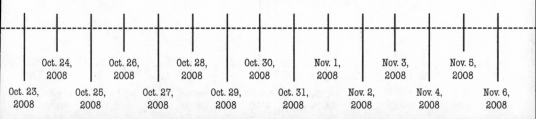

Oct. 23, 2008 · Oct. 24, 2008 · Oct. 25, 2008 · Oct. 26, 2008 · Oct. 27, 2008 · Oct. 28, 2008 · Oct. 29, 2008 · Oct. 30, 2008 · Oct. 31, 2008 · Nov. 1, 2008 · Nov. 2, 2008 · Nov. 3, 2008 · Nov. 4, 2008 · Nov. 5, 2008 · Nov. 6, 2008

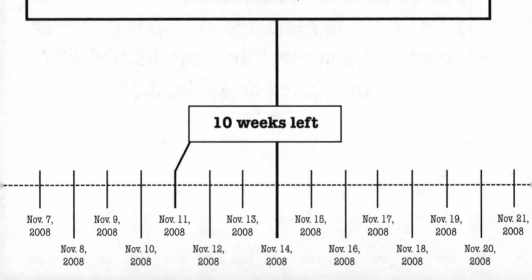

Secretary of State Condoleezza Rice's birthday.
"We need a common enemy to unite us."
—Condoleezza Rice

Born on November 14, 1954

10 weeks left

Nov. 7,
2008

Nov. 8,
2008

Nov. 9,
2008

Nov. 10,
2008

Nov. 11,
2008

Nov. 12,
2008

Nov. 13,
2008

Nov. 14,
2008

Nov. 15,
2008

Nov. 16,
2008

Nov. 17,
2008

Nov. 18,
2008

Nov. 19,
2008

Nov. 20,
2008

Nov. 21,
2008

"We want our teachers to be trained so they can meet the obligations, their obligations as teachers. We want them to know how to teach the science of reading. In order to make sure there's not this kind of federal-federal cufflink."

March 30, 2000, Milwaukee, Wisconsin

"I think it's very important for the American president to mean what he says. That's why I understand that the enemy could misread what I say. That's why I try to be as clearly as I can."

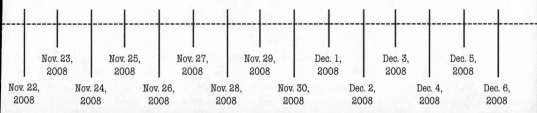

Nov. 22, 2008
Nov. 23, 2008
Nov. 24, 2008
Nov. 25, 2008
Nov. 26, 2008
Nov. 27, 2008
Nov. 28, 2008
Nov. 29, 2008
Nov. 30, 2008
Dec. 1, 2008
Dec. 2, 2008
Dec. 3, 2008
Dec. 4, 2008
Dec. 5, 2008
Dec. 6, 2008

"In other words, I don't think people ought to be compelled to make the decision which they think is best for their family."

*December 11, 2002, Washington, D.C.,
regarding smallpox vaccinations*

"Justice was being delivered to a man who defied that gift from the Almighty to the people of Iraq."

December 15, 2003, Washington, D.C.

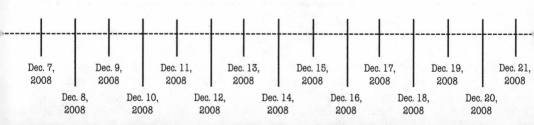

Dec. 7, 2008   Dec. 9, 2008   Dec. 11, 2008   Dec. 13, 2008   Dec. 15, 2008   Dec. 17, 2008   Dec. 19, 2008   Dec. 21, 2008

Dec. 8, 2008   Dec. 10, 2008   Dec. 12, 2008   Dec. 14, 2008   Dec. 16, 2008   Dec. 18, 2008   Dec. 20, 2008

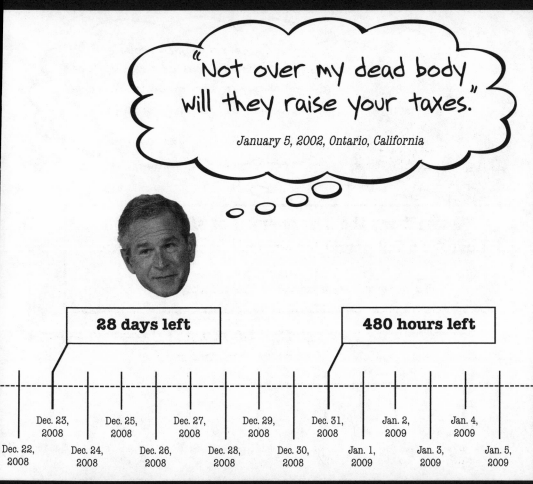

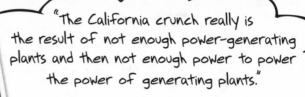

"The California crunch really is the result of not enough power-generating plants and then not enough power to power the power of generating plants."

January 14, 2001, The New York Times

"I would say the best moment of all was when I caught a 7.5 pound largemouth bass in my lake."

May 7, 2006 in German newspaper
Bild am Sonntag about the best moment of his presidency

THE LAST DAY!

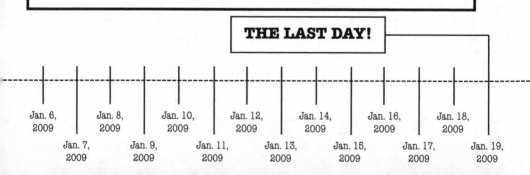

Jan. 6, 2009
Jan. 7, 2009
Jan. 8, 2009
Jan. 9, 2009
Jan. 10, 2009
Jan. 11, 2009
Jan. 12, 2009
Jan. 13, 2009
Jan. 14, 2009
Jan. 15, 2009
Jan. 16, 2009
Jan. 17, 2009
Jan. 18, 2009
Jan. 19, 2009